MANNING: ANGLICAN AND CATHOLIC

MANNING :
Anglican and Catholic

Edited by

JOHN FITZSIMONS

GREENWOOD PRESS, PUBLISHERS
WESTPORT, CONNECTICUT

Library of Congress Cataloging in Publication Data

Fitzsimons, John, 1913–   ed.
    Manning, Anglican and Catholic.

    Reprint of the 1951 ed. published by Burns, Oates,
London.
    1. Manning, Henry Edward, Cardinal, 1800–1892.
2. Cardinals—England—Biography. I. Title.
[BX4705.M3F5 1979]   262'.135'0924 [B]   78-11571
ISBN 0-313-21005-5

NIHIL OBSTAT: EDVARDVS MAHONEY, S.T.D.
CENSOR DEPVTATVS
IMPRIMATVR: E. MORROGH BERNARD
VICARIVS GENERALIS
WESTMONASTERII: DIE XXII FEBRVARII MCMLI

First published 1951 by Burns Oates & Washbourne, Ltd.

Reprinted with the permission of Burns & Oates, Ltd.

Reprinted in 1979 by Greenwood Press, Inc.
51 Riverside Avenue, Westport, CT 06880

Printed in the United States of America

10 9 8 7 6 5 4 3 2 1

PREFACE

THIS year sees the centenary of one of the most important events of the Church's history in England in the nineteenth century, for on Passion Sunday, April 6, 1851, Henry Edward Manning, lately Archdeacon of Chichester and Rector of Lavington, made his submission to Rome in the church of the Jesuit Fathers at Farm Street. The present collection of essays, while not pretending to be the full-length biography that is still needed, is meant to commemorate the event with a just but critical appreciation of his life and interests.

The book is in two parts, dealing respectively with Manning's life and interests, which are joined by essays on Manning's friends and on his relations with Newman. While it may seem unfortunate to stress in this way the Manning-Newman breach, this arrangement seemed the only way in which their relations could be dealt with, and both essays are written by Sir Shane Leslie, who has continued his researches into the Manning archives and here includes new material discovered since the publication of his biography.

The importance of the first essay—and the justification of what may seem its disproportionate length—is that Manning's character is nowhere revealed more clearly than in his slow and painful progress from the Anglican to the Catholic Church. His attempts at objective evaluation, his emotional conversion years before his intellectual conviction—these are keys to a character which, while not being immediately attractive, is by its very humanity entitled to admiration and respect. Fr Chapeau, who is a Professor in the Faculty of Letters in the Catholic University of the West at Angers, has been working on the Manning Papers for the last twenty years, and has ready for the press what will probably be the definitive history of Manning as an Anglican—the first volume of what will eventually be a complete ' Life.' After Manning's conversion the focus of his activities was the foundation he had made at Bayswater of the Oblates of St Charles, and this

is dealt with by Fr Denis Ward, who is Rector of the Oblates'
house at Kensal New Town. Finally, the story of Manning
as Archbishop of Westminster and the growth and changes in
the archdiocese during his reign are covered by Dr Gordon
Albion, Secretary of the Catholic Records Society.

The second part of the book covers the chief interests and
activities of Manning during the twenty-seven years that he
occupied the See of Westminster. Fr Purdy, until recently
Professor of Ecclesiastical History at St Edmund's, Ware,
writes of the part that Manning played as one of the leaders
of the ' Opportunists ' in the definition of Papal Infallibility,
the doctrine which years before Manning had found to be
one of the chief stumbling blocks to his conversion. Two
writers who have made the nineteenth century their special
province, Mr Christopher Howard, who is a Lecturer at
King's College, London, and Dr Denis Gwynn, who is a
Professor at University College, Cork, contribute essays on
two of the chief preoccupations of the latter half of that
century: Education and the Irish Question. It would seem
that Manning's interventions in the latter were more happy
than his sins of omission in the former, despite his devotion to
the cause of Catholic education. In the evening of his life
Manning devoted more and more of his time and still unfailing
energies to what is called ' the social question ' and made
various contributions which were not without influence on the
development of Catholic social doctrine in its early, Leonine
days. This, and in particular his part in the famous London
Dock Strike of 1889, is described in the essay contributed by
the Editor. Finally, Mgr Davis, the Vice-Rector of Oscott
College, writes of Manning's contribution to our spiritual
literature. His piety was reduced by Strachey to little more
than Evangelism, broad and low, with more than a hint of
a traumatic childhood experience. His spiritual writings, and
more particularly his classic work on the priesthood, give the
lie to this and show the riches of his inner life to which the
well-known ascetic features bore testimony.

JOHN FITZSIMONS

March, 1951

CONTENTS

I

MANNING THE ANGLICAN

By Alphonse Chapeau

O NE should perhaps warn the reader at the outset that he will find here a very different Manning from the usual portrait. Manning the Anglican has been overshadowed by the picture of the emaciated face with thin lips compressed in stern command, the eyes seeming already lost in the contemplation of things above. That certainly is the ' People's Cardinal ' of the ' *misereor super turbam*,' and he is in strange contrast with Manning the distinguished parson. Manning the archdeacon, his face illuminated by thought or overshadowed by frustration, although it betrayed already his interior life, was still very much that of a man of the world. Only the last picture of him, at the altar, detached and immolated, makes him completely spiritual. But this is in reality the first picture of his new life and of a new world. There lies the key to the interior drama of the conversion that was accomplished in Manning's Anglican days.

He was born into a rich upper-middle-class family. His father, William Manning, was a member of Parliament for thirty-two years and for some time a Governor of the Bank of England, and in the Tory party represented the high finance of the City. Henry Edward Manning had a happy childhood, both at Copped Hall, Totteridge, where he was born on July 15, 1808, and at Combe Bank, Sundridge, near Sevenoaks, where the family went to live after 1815. His mother taught him his letters, the rudiments of Latin grammar, piety and the fear of God. Above all she instilled in him the fear of God: ' the big book in which God wrote down everything that we did wrong ' and ' the lake that burneth with fire and brimstone ' filled the imagination of the sensitive child and remained with him all his life. The book of hymns of Mrs Barbauld introduced him to the story of the creation of the world. The rest of his religious background was that of his environment— his family was strictly Church of England, ' high and dry.'

The two successive Rectors of Sundridge were Dr Wordsworth and the Rev. Mr D'Oyly, 'and believe me,' wrote Manning, 'they were very dry.' The piety of the family was strongly Evangelical, as Mr Manning was much influenced by his cousin William Wilberforce, who also persuaded him, against his business interests, to join the Abolitionist campaign. But his children were baptized by bishops, and Henry rode his pony in the park at Combe Bank with the Bishop of Lincoln. It was understood that when he was older he would take Orders and he accepted the idea, although he was far from pleased when his brothers called him ' the parson.'

He entered Harrow in 1822 and found it difficult. His preparation had not been sufficient, and he was on his own, 'literally without religious guidance or formation' in an atmosphere that was often brutal, surrounded by the perils of adolescence. ' I had faith, a great fear of hell, and said my prayers: beyond, all was a blank. . . . It was not a good time with me . . . God held me by my will against my will. . . . Harrow was my greatest danger.' He was not outstanding in his studies, but made his mark by his character and by his prowess at sport—he was captain of the Cricket XI. Because of his leadership he was called ' the General.' The death of his sister Harriet, in whom he was wont to confide, left a gap in his life which was filled by his brother-in-law, J. L. Anderdon, who, although sixteen years older, became his adviser and moral and intellectual mentor. Only with him could Henry Edward forget his natural timidity and overcome his reserve.

When the time came for him to go up to Oxford, he spent nine months at Paulshot with a crammer, Canon William Fisher, and while there made great progress, particularly in acquiring a method of working. He went up in October 1827 and entered Balliol, but was in no hurry to settle down to hard work. He rode, played cricket and rowed—but for his health would have got his Blue in rowing—and even went in for boxing. He soon had the reputation of being ' one of the three most handsome men in Oxford.' However, he was too fond of his books to neglect them and saw his tutor, Herman Merivale, three times a week. At the same time John Anderdon kept encouraging him to work and made him enthusiastic about Foster and his *Decision of Character*. At this time he made his first important decision when he wrote to his father that ' the thought of being a clergyman had utterly passed from me. . . . It is impossible.' This was one weight less on his mind, but he was greatly bothered with his health. He had caught cold one day at cricket at Harrow and now suffered from disturbing attacks of asthma. He never recovered completely from this and had to have special treatment which continued throughout his life.

He began to make his mark in the Union, became interested in speaking and in politics, and showed that he could speak on any subject ' with infallible ease and sureness of expression.' He was elected to succeed Samuel Wilberforce as President of the Union, but at the height of his ambitions had to refuse. The family fortunes were shaky and he had to look to his future. So he had to give up the Union in order to concentrate on working for his Finals. He weighed his chances and organized his work. ' I never knew you undertake anything you did not do,' said his mother. Along with Gladstone, J. R. Hope and W. Hamilton he worked with Charles Wordsworth and spent his vacation at Oxford; but to do this required a great effort of will.

To say so and to do so is equally an act of volition. . . . If my hopes are ever realized, if the aspirations I dare entertain are ever met, I shall stand in many a more perilous position; such as will require not only intellectual requirements, but moral courage to collect and employ them. I *will try and take a First in this*, if not *in litteris humanioribus*.

He did get a First, and had already written to Anderdon ' I do not expect so much as to falter in the Schools: this is a moral not an intellectual principle.' His degree was an outward recognition of the more important inner victory that he had won over himself.

In winter the blow fell—the house of Manning and Anderdon failed. Henry Edward had to look immediately for a post, and became a clerk in the Colonial Office through the good offices of a friend of his father. He had to turn his back on the future that lay before him, with all its possibilities abruptly cut off. After some time he seems to have passed through some kind of crisis, in the course of which he had an ' interior illumination ' which caused what he was later to call his ' first conversion.' Actually the change had been coming slowly and almost unconsciously for some time. Mr Anderdon had had his share in it, but it was due even more to a Miss Bevan, the sister of a college friend. He had passed part of his vacations with them at Trent Park. The family was Puritan and the daughter of the house an ardent apostle of Evangelicalism. With Manning she had a voluminous correspondence, took him to open-air meetings, and became his ' spiritual mother,' turning his thoughts to higher realities. ' Heavenly ambitions are not closed against you,' she told him, and she watched over and helped ' a work of grace going on in his heart.' And then the light dawned.

All this [Manning wrote later] made a new thought spring up in me—not to be a clergyman in the sense of my old destiny, but to give up the world and to live for God and for souls. . . . I had been long praying much and going habitually to churches. It was a turning point in my life. . . . It was as surely a call from God as all that He has given me since. . . . It was a call *ad veritatem et ad seipsum*. As such I listed it and followed it.

Immediately he resigned from the Colonial Office. A Fellowship was vacant at Merton, and he applied for it. On April 8, 1832, he was voted the Fellowship and so returned to the quiet gardens of Oxford to prepare for Orders. On December 23 of the same year he was ordained deacon by Bishop Bagot, and on Christmas Day preached his first sermon, in the church at Cuddesdon, on the text from Isaias: *Surge illuminare Jerusalem*. A singular prophecy of things to come.

On January 5, 1833, he took up his first appointment as curate to the Rev. John Sargent, Rector of Lavington and Graffham in Sussex. It was intended to be an interim post until the ordination of Henry Wilberforce, the younger brother of Samuel who, in 1828, had married Emily, the eldest of the Sargent girls. Manning's father was an uncle by marriage of the Sargents, and Mrs Carey, Manning's half-sister, lived at Graffham. However, Manning had been only four months in this earthly paradise when the Rector died, on May 3, and his mother gave to Manning the family living. On June 9, Bishop Maltby of Chichester ordained him priest in the chapel of Lincoln's Inn and on November 7, in the little chapel at Lavington, Samuel Wilberforce blessed his marriage with Caroline, the third of the Sargent girls—the second, Mary, was already engaged to Henry Wilberforce. And so he settled down at Lavington which over the years he came to love dearly. ' I loved the little church under the green hill-side,' he wrote in *England and Christendom*, ' where the morning and evening prayers and the music of the English Bible for seventeen years became a part of my soul. Nothing is more beautiful in the natural order, and if there were no eternal world I could have made it my home.'

Nobody could have been more zealous than the young Rector of Lavington. Every morning, dressed in his white surplice, he rang the bell himself, and in the evening he put his father's coat over his surplice to go and say Evensong. His piety was sincere, and he did all he could to restore in his church whatever would help the fervour of his flock. But at the same time he had to look to his own education, and pass through a strange and dangerous territory of the spirit. He has left us a description of the state of his beliefs in 1833:

I had profound faith in the Holy Trinity and the Incarnation, in the Redemption by the Passion of our Lord, and in the work of the Holy Spirit and the conversion of the soul. As to the Church I had no definite conception. . . . In truth, I had thought and read myself out of contact with every system known to me. . . . Of the Catholic Church I knew nothing . . . I held intensely to the ' Word of God,' and the work of souls.

As yet the problem of the position of the Established Church did not exist for him—the atmosphere of his piety was Evangelical because he was bound to it by personal attachments and by feeling. He was in fact, as he was to admit later, nothing more or less than a ' Pietist.' He ' preached to the poor in church, and in their homes.' He knew them all and made nearly all his visits on foot in his cassock; he also kept an up-to-date census of the parish. His wife helped him in all his charities and was often the inspirer of his piety. Alas, after less than four years of married life, on July 24, 1837, she died at the age of twenty-five of consumption. Once more Providence had caused an abrupt change in Manning's life, and called for complete renunciation on his part. This was the worst blow of all, and the wound remained with Manning to the end of his days, although he concealed it completely. Nevertheless one may fix this date as the occasion of his second conversion, his death to the world and his detachment from things of the earth. Three days after his wife's death he wrote to Gladstone: ' God has been graciously pleased to lead me into a way that is a desert, and to bid me serve Him with entire surrender of myself.' Ten years later, in the face of death, when he looked back to what he called his ' visitations of grace,' and he spoke of ' God's special mercies,' ' chief agents in my conversion,' the date 1837 recurred again and again: ' chastized,' ' bruised,' ' awakened.' He only opened his heart on this lifelong pain to one man, Herbert Vaughan, his spiritual son and eventual successor—his last words on earth, on January 14, 1892.

Even during the first four years of his pastoral ministry he had begun to move towards Catholicism. He had considered the Evangelical piety of the Sargent family and of the Wilber-forces and thought it imperfect and partial, a compromise with the truth, and out of harmony with the New Testament. It was clear to him that if one deliberately did not teach the whole of revealed truth, then inevitably sooner or later one would be forced to reject some essential truths. There was another question too that troubled him: ' What right have you to be teaching, admonishing, reforming, rebuking others? By what authority do you lift the latch of a poor man's door and enter and sit down and begin to instruct or correct him? . . . If I was not a messenger sent from God, I was an intruder and an impertinent.' Thus he arrived at the great question of his time—is there a Church? Where is it? What does it do?

Manning had been a priest three months, to the day, when the first of the *Tracts for the Times* appeared. He read them regularly from the outset; the Wilberforces and S. F. Wood, his intimate friend who was a member of the ' Oriel group,' kept him posted. But, while he adopted the main lines and the essentials of their doctrine, he kept his independence. However, he accepted the invitation of Newman to join their working group, and began to study the Fathers. In 1835 St Vincent of Lérins and Tradition became his chief preoccupation,

at the time when Newman was looking for a firm foundation for his *Via Media*. On July 7, 1835, he preached the
Archdeacon's Visitation Sermon in the cathedral at Chichester
on 'The English Church: its Succession and Witness for
Christ.' He developed the Tractarian doctrine of the Apostolic
Succession, a subject which he had told Newman absorbed him
and which he wished to pursue further. He was ranged with
the High Churchmen, and as such began to be attacked, while
at the same time he was defending the Catholicity of the
Church of England against Wiseman. He kept up his study
of Tradition, not because it was fashionable, nor to please
Newman and Pusey, but in order to find a satisfactory basis
for his own ministry and teaching. 'These are the witnesses
of the mind of the Church at all times,' he said of the Fathers.
'How far am I in harmony with them?' St Vincent of Lérins
gave him the key and principles for his study, and he proposed
to Newman a *Catena Patrum* on the subject of the Catholic
Tradition. 'It is curious you should mention the subject,'
wrote Newman on October 18, 1836, '(It was) the very next
subject I meant to have taken.' Manning's *Catena Patrum*,
with additions by Charles Marriott, was published as *Tract 78*
on February 2, 1837. Manning then agreed to collaborate
in Pusey's projected 'Library of the Fathers,' and offered to be
responsible for the works of St Justin Martyr, because he was
one of the earliest and Manning (like Newman) wished to
study the Fathers in chronological order.

But by now it is the Spring of 1837 and he had begun to
climb his Calvary. The death of his wife brought him nearer
to Newman, but he was unable to reply to Newman's
affectionate words of sympathy until three months later. 'I
feel the absolute need of full employment,' he wrote to Newman.
'All I can do now is to keep at work. There is a sort of rush
in my mind when unoccupied I can hardly bear.'

Fortunately, Dr Maltby, a Low Churchman whom Manning
had visited as little as possible, was succeeded as Bishop of
Chichester by Dr Otter. Manning was a frequent visitor
henceforward at the Palace, and was appointed Rural Dean
of Midhurst and later became Diocesan Secretary of Education.

In 1837 came the first steps of the Government to reform the
Church, and hence the first conflicts between Church and

State. In the diocese of Chichester Manning took the lead in
resisting these encroachments of the civil power which to him
meant nothing less than ' the virtual extinction of the polity
of the Church.' He fought for the re-establishment of the old
diocesan synods and provincial councils. But little could be
done in the face of the apathy, the lack of interest, even the
ignorance and opposition of the bishops. It was at this time
that Manning published his *Letter to the Bishop of Chichester on
the Principle of the Ecclesiastical Commission.* Newman corrected
the proofs and said that he had ' nothing to find fault with.'
Manning had already written: ' The present line of policy
must make it, sooner or later, impossible to communicate with
the established religion. No man can know how great the
schism will be till the separation has begun. And when it
does begin, it will let out the very life of our present religious
system. It will be a rending asunder of soul and body.'
Manning did not know that he was even then prophesying his
own ' rending asunder,' what he called ' a death.'

Another opportunity occurred for him to declare solemnly
his position, and not only for himself but for all those who now
followed him and modelled their views on his. Bishop Otter
invited him to preach the Visitation Sermon on June 13, 1838.
Newman had stated his idea of the *Via Media* in a strangely
indecisive way which made it seem more like a system that he
wished to test. But for Manning ambiguity of this kind was
impossible. ' Is the Anglican Church,' he asked, ' faithful to
the Apostles' doctrine? Is there identity between the Anglican
Rule of Faith and the faith of the primitive Church?' The
answer had to be in the affirmative. In his sermon, *The Rule
of Faith,* he praised the work of the Reformation (he judged
this necessary after the publication of Froude's *Remains*) and
at the same time attacked the Liberals and Low Churchmen
who laid claim to ' an immediate guidance of that same Spirit
by Whom the Scriptures were dictated,' and substitute themselves for the Church in the work of witness.

Men are now again reduced to the necessity of making a
further choice [he concluded] between that which was the
faith of the English Church . . . and spurious Protestantism.
. . . The temper of these days is arrayed in the most
irreconcilable warfare against the rule of faith . . . and

men have acquired an impatience of any fixed standard of religious truth external to the mind.

The Sermon caused a great deal of impassioned discussion and Manning was subjected to violent attacks. Against these he reacted vehemently, even to the extent of injuring his health. He published an *Appendix* to the Sermon which constituted a summary of Anglican theology as well as a proof of his position. One effect of this was that the Evangelical perodical *The Record* spoke of his ' apostasy ' and ' fall from the Gospel.' For it his treason lay in opposing ' antiquity ' to private judgement, and his statement that the rejection of universal Tradition would lead to schism and to Socinianism filled it with horror: ' The Sermon was bad enough. The Appendix was abominable.'

Nevertheless Manning continued to maintain his uneasy balance in the *Via Media*, and having smote his opponents on the left he now turned his attention to the right, namely Wiseman. Wiseman had already in the April 1838 number of *The Dublin Review* denounced the ' two watchwords of the Oxford writers: antiquity and authority,' and had shown how all their efforts tended to restore in the Anglican Church those principles and practices of the primitive Church that the Reformation had destroyed but which the Catholics had preserved. Now, in the October issue, he attacked ' the claims of the Anglican Church to the rights and privileges of apostolical succession.' In reply Manning tried desperately to unite in a single condemnation the ' Roman rule,' the interpretation of a living Church and the New rule of Popular Protestantism, the private judgement of the individual. They both, said he, put the ' living judge ' above the ' written rule of Tradition.' Now for the first time appear from his pen the fateful words of ' the Roman doctrine of Infallibility.' It was for him his greatest obstacle, and from now on he did not falter until he had overcome it, and indeed ultimately contributed more than any other single individual to defining this fundamental doctrine. It is interesting to note that he proposed certain theories that Newman was later to make the basis of *Tract 90*, that ' the Articles are not new theological determinations . . . but depositions of evidence exhibiting interpretations that have obtained credit from the beginning.'

He also quoted his great author, St Vincent of Lérins, on *profectus religionis*, religious development, a theme which Newman was later to expand.

Despite all this exterior activity of controversy Manning was turning more and more to his interior life, and already the main lines of it can be seen from his notes in his meditation book:

> God, the ultimate resting place of men. . . . The note of sanctity, the chief note of the Church—The Holy Ghost a Teacher. . . . ' I am with you always ' . . . The spiritual presence pledged: 1. The Church indefectible; 2. The gift of regeneration ever new.

For himself he drew certain conclusions :

> All sects a section within and without the Church. . . Separation from good people sometimes necessary. . . . The restoration of spiritual and ascetic obedience, the restoration of Catholicism, now inevitable. . . . The Church the only reality in the world.

For the sake of his health he left England to spend the winter of 1838–9 in Italy. ' Henry Manning is gone to Rome for the winter,' wrote Samuel Wilberforce. ' The Bishop of London wickedly suggests he thought he had been there ever since publishing his last volume of sermons ' (i.e. *The Rule of Faith* and the *Appendix*). Manning arrived in the Eternal City on December 10 and he and Gladstone went to hear all the sermons they could, and called on Wiseman, Rector of the Venerabile. In fact Manning went to see him several times. In March he went to Naples, then Sicily and Malta, and returned by Lombardy, the Tyrol and the Rhine. He had tried to convince himself of ' Roman corruption ' but returned instead with his idea of the ' infallibility of the Church ' stronger than ever: ' Is any promised or no? If yes, where?' This was the inevitable outcome of the Rule of Faith. Again and again he returned to the problem: ' I am ready to believe that in the main the Church Catholic *has not* erred: and *will* not err: but I dare not say *can* not.' The essential basis was missing. He still wished to build everything on the artificial basis of the *Via Media*, which inspired his confident view of the ' English Mission ': ' God's special favour watched over our succession and favoured it. . . . The destiny of the English Church to be the centre of a new system.'

Back at Lavington he turned to Newman for help, but Newman was strangely reticent and this he could not understand. He gave the impression of a sudden weakening and an inexplicable leaning towards Rome. He did not know and he could not guess that Newman had ' seen his first ghost, face to face.' Manning was once again caught up in manifold activities. He protested against the ' Cathedral Act ' of Lord John Russell in another letter to the Bishop of Chichester entitled *The Preservation of Unendowed Canonries*. But Bishop Otter, one of the few who had remained in the fray throughout the long Parliamentary session, was worn out with the effort and died in August 1839. The new Bishop was Dr Shuttleworth, Warden of New College, a Low Churchman and an anti-Tractarian. Yet at his first large diocesan meeting held at Brighton where Manning spoke on matters relating to education he was won by him. He took Manning back with him and on the way promised to make him archdeacon. A few weeks later the aged Archdeacon Webber resigned and on December 24, 1840, Manning succeeded him as Archdeacon of Chichester. He was not yet thirty-three, and was full of confidence in the future.

His faith in his Church remained unshaken, although his visit to Italy had made him more careful in defining it:

That I abhor and tremble at Romish errors, God is witness [he wrote to Gladstone on April 17, 1841], but I cannot refuse to sympathize with what is high and true and lovely in their system. And as for the hollow false soulless shapeless no-system of Protestantism I can yield to it neither the homage of reason nor of affection. The English Church is a real substantive Catholic body capable of development and all perfection—able to lick up and absorb all that is true and beautiful in all Christendom into itself—and this is our problem.

And, a few days later :

I have been thinking much of what we have said about developing the Catholic element of the English Church. If we had but the visible undeniable note of sanctity upon us, nothing should resist us.

He now began to work to bring this about. In two years he made a Visitation of the one hundred and thirty parishes in his archdeaconry; he organized Rural Chapters at which he normally presided himself; and every year all the deans met with him at Lavington. Untiringly, he set himself to restore interior and exterior discipline and to promote to the highest degree the devotion and the spiritual life of the clergy and the laity. The sermons that he published had considerable success and his influence was spread far and wide.

He was nominated Select Preacher for the University of Oxford. Three days after his first sermon in Newman's pulpit, *Tract 90* appeared. Manning was not involved in the violent repercussions because he did not belong to Oxford— he was only a visitor. Moreover, he found it difficult to understand Newman's dilemma, and in fact his own doctrinal position was nearer to Pusey than to Newman. Nothing distracted him from his chief objective. On Trinity Sunday he preached the Ordination Sermon in Chichester Cathedral and took as his subject ' The Moral Design of the Apostolic Ministry '—the same theme of sanctity. In his charge, given in July, he insisted on this once again, while adding a pressing appeal for unity. The anniversary of his bereavement he passed in retreat and meditation, and called it a ' holy week.' He confided in his colleague, Archdeacon Hare of Lewes, and expounded his position to him:

> I find myself a member of a branch of the Catholic Church which has personal identity with the Church of the Apostles. The properties of this personal identity are a knowledge of the pure truth and a power to do in Christ's name the same acts for the reconciling of man to God. My life's work therefore is not to innovate upon this basis, but to develop it. Again—the area in which this is to be wrought is the jurisdiction both as Pastor and as Archdeacon assigned to me by the same hand which grafted me into His Church. . . . What we desire is to reunite and develop the Church as a great living energizing reality.

This was the great new idea that now possessed him, unity, the essential mark and indispensable condition of the Catholic Church. Unfortunately the course of events was soon to make this seem more remote than ever. First there was the 'fearful business' (as Newman called it) of the Anglo-Prussian bishopric of Jerusalem, an attempt at a Luthero-Anglican Church. Then there followed at Oxford, on the occasion of the contest for the Chair of Poetry, the first major defeat of the Tractarians as a party. The leader of the anti-Tractarians was rewarded by being appointed to the see of Chichester.

Nevertheless Manning published his treatise on *The Unity of the Church*, and dedicated it to Gladstone. It was 'the best apologia that he could make for the Anglican Church.' By now he was surrounded by disturbance and instability: Sibthorpe and Bernard Smith had defaulted, while Newman, S. F. Wood, Lockhart and J. R. Hope are in danger of defection. Gladstone was immune (for ever, unfortunately) because of the circles in which he moved, but Miss Gladstone had already gone over to Rome. Manning tried to clarify his ideas in a treatise which he left unfinished amongst his notes, and which he called *Religio Anglo-Catholici*. It begins with the statement: 'My allegiance to the Church in England is on the hypothesis of its agreement and unity with the Church universal,' and then he hastens to add: 'Of that agreement I may play the judge if I will: but I shall be wiser if I forbear.' He then notes the practical reasons for his loyalty:

I could not leave the Church of England without sin. . . . I dare not separate myself from the Church of England which is the visible channel of grace to the English people . . . their way of salvation . . . de facto they have no other? I dare not leave off to labour for them.

It is interesting to note the objectives that he sets himself:

There are three things for which I am prepared to labour with all the little strength I have.—First, to restore to the Church of England whatsoever may be wanting of Catholic doctrine, opinion, discipline and practice.—Next, to win Romanists by fair dealing and charitable interpretation from the points which differentiate them from us.—And lastly, to bring on the union of the Churches of England and Rome on the basis of Catholic truth.

Further on he writes of the sentimental ties which bind him to the Church of England and which were to cause him so much sorrow when the time came to break them:

> The first love of my soul is to the Church of England, my mother in the Spirit. . . . The Church of England is so interwoven with the life of this English race of which I am, that I cannot separate them in my affections.

Nevertheless he goes on:

> Next to the Church of England there is nothing between heaven and earth that commands from me so strong and fond a love as the Church of Rome.

He followed this with an astonishing revelation of a secret admiration for the Church when he still knew so little about her:

> Her sanctity, her deeds of love, . . . her universal missions: her worldwide communion: her majesty, grandeur and reality, in the vision of history and in the strife of earthly kingdoms: all these and the charity which binds me to the 140,000,000 of my brethren in Christ draw the liveliest and purest affection of my heart to the Roman Church.

One can see the shadow of Newman behind the hand that went on to write: ' I would not outrage it, nor slander it, nor revile it for the most dazzling bribe.' However, the day was near at hand when Manning, caught up by sudden and violent emotion and fearing a mortal danger, would denounce and attack Rome.

In 1843 Newman retracted ' all the hard things he had said against the Church of Rome,' thus ' breaking the *Via Media* to pieces.' Then in May, Pusey was condemned for a sermon he had preached on the Blessed Sacrament and was forbidden to preach for two years within the University. After the conversion of Lockhart, Newman, weighed down with episcopal condemnations, resigned and retired into a lay community. On September 25 when Newman bade farewell to his friends at Littlemore Manning was at York, but as soon as he got back to Lavington he wrote to Newman to express his ' affection and the real part that he took in his afflictions,' and at the same time expressed the desire ' to know more of your intimate thoughts in order the better to understand.' Newman did not hesitate to disclose the state of his soul to ' a friend who had

every claim upon me ' and wrote on October 14: ' It is felt that
I am a foreign material and cannot assimilate with the Church
of England. . . . I fear that I must confess that, in proportion
as I think the English Church is showing herself intrinsically
and radically alien from Catholic principles, so do I feel the
difficulties of defending her claims to be a branch of the
Catholic Church.' As Manning insisted on clarification, he
wrote eleven days later: ' I must tell you frankly that it is not
from disappointment, irritation or impatience, that I have,
whether rightly or wrongly, resigned St Mary's: but because
I think the Church of Rome the Catholic Church, and ours
not part of the Catholic Church because not in communion
with Rome.' He added: ' You may make what use of my
letters you think right.' Manning was overcome, but would
communicate the terrible secret to no one except Gladstone,
who ' staggers to and fro like a drunken man, and is at his wit's
end.' Then he thought of its effect on the Church, and wrote
on November 2: ' The possession of this sad and heavy
secret binds us first to endeavour to disperse the subject of it
without explosion, and next to provide *ne quid detrimenti capiat
Ecclesia*. This last is to me a grave question. We are responsible to the Church for this knowledge.' He thought of his own
position and decided that he would be a bad shepherd and an
impostor if he did not warn those who put their confidence
in him of the danger that threatened. He informed Pusey
of Newman's letters and commented:

> I feel to have been for four years on the brink of I know
> not what; all the while persuading myself and others that
> all was well—that none were so true and steadfast to the
> English Church. . . . I feel as if I had been a deceiver
> speaking lies (God knows, not in hypocrisy). And this
> has caused a sort of shock in my mind that makes me
> tremble. . . . I have been using his books, defending and
> endeavouring to spread the system which carried this
> dreadful secret at its heart. . . . I am now reduced to the
> painful, saddening, sickening necessity of saying what I
> feel about Rome.

The occasion for this was at hand, providentially so he
thought. His turn to preach at Oxford fell on Sunday,
November 5. He spoke in praise of the Reformation in order

to uphold against Rome the position that Newman had deserted and which Pusey seemed no longer dare to defend. The position is clear—it is not he but Newman who has changed. At first Newman was displeased and showed temper but then understood, and soon after wrote to Manning again to renew his protestation of affection: ' It would be strange if I had the heart to blame others who are honest in maintaining what I am abandoning.' Manning was greatly disturbed, and he could not help thinking of a ' formidable contingency more or less remote—maybe indefinitely near or indefinitely far,' and he wrote to Gladstone (December 29): ' I believe I speak the truth when I say that the thought of him has driven everything else out of my mind. . . . It has made me perfectly absent about other things.'

Up to now we have followed Manning step by step in the first part of his life up to the moment at the beginning of 1845 when he seems to be the providential successor of those who have hitherto led the Anglo-Catholics. It is not possible to follow him further in his external activities. But this is not necessary, for from now on the drama of his conversion is transferred almost completely to the interior life of his soul. The great events which followed are well known: the condemnation of Ward, the forced resignation of Oakeley who had stood by him, their reception in the Catholic Church, followed by the disciples of Littlemore, and finally Newman himself on October 9, 1845.

In all these conflicts Manning had a part. He wrote to Newman in February that he was coming to see him at Oxford: ' I owe to you more than to anyone living, and the thought of a difference from you in anything, much more in vital things, has weighed on me, I may say all day long since October of last year. It is a relief to me to do anything which joins me to you where I can, and to call back again the thoughts of other days.'

And so he waited. He engaged in a long controversy with Oakeley, he exchanged letters with Pusey, Gladstone and Keble, and with Robert Wilberforce. He admitted to the last-named that he was ' all anxious and over sensitive,' although ' nothing can shake my belief of the presence of Christ in our Church and sacrament: I feel incapable of doubting it.' But he was forced to add: 'Our theology is a chaos, we have no principles, no form, no order, no structure or science.' When Newman wrote to tell him the fateful news of his conversion he replied: 'If I knew what words would express my heartfelt love of you and keep my own conscience pure, I would use them. . . . Only believe always that I love you. If we may never meet again in life at the same altar, may our intercession for each other, day by day, meet in the court of Heaven.' To Gladstone he repeated the same sentiments: 'What do I not owe him? No living man has so powerfully affected me: and there is no mind I have so reverenced. . . . His whole course is fearful to me—and though I seem to feel a clear and undoubting conviction that he has by some mysterious inclination swerved from truth in the points which divide us—his course has about it a strange fascination.' He fought against discouragement, and found an odd basis for hope: 'I cannot but feel that it is a fact which must have its consequences, ethical and intellectual, in our relation to Rome: and decidedly for good. They must learn to understand and appreciate us more truly: and I trust love us more, which they have done but little as yet.'

But the Movement was finished at Oxford where Pusey was still the leader, though alone and isolated. The influence of Keble was not felt in external affairs but rather the attraction of his piety and character. In practical affairs the lead had been taken by a number of men in London, Upton Richards of Margaret Street and Bennett of St Barnabas'. Manning was not involved and declared himself 'less and less able to enter into Pusey's mode of speaking and judging,' although he admitted that it was 'a painful and almost a hateful task to say anything of one who is so tender, loving and devoted.' But he realized that this was the end of a phase, for he wrote in his journal: 'I have taken my last act with those who are moving in Oxford. Henceforward I shall endeavour by God's help to act by myself without any alliance. My duty is to live and die striving to edify the Church in my own sphere.'

From the doctrinal point of view he was horrified at what seemed to be Pusey's position: 'to take half on trust and half to try.' He could not tolerate a half faith, and wanted a

position that was quite clear. Hence he was anxious to steer
his followers away from dangers, and so ' I was regarded and
even censured as slow to advance . . . cautious to excess,
morbidly moderate as one said.' His austerity, zeal, piety and
firmness attracted many to him, and the expression ' Safe as
Manning ' became almost a proverb in those troublous times.
Yet none of the friends who consulted him, not Pusey, nor
Keble, nor Gladstone, nor Hope, not even his intimates
Dodsworth and Robert Wilberforce, had any suspicion of the
struggle that was going on in his soul. For since the great
shock of the summer of 1845 he had turned in on himself, on
himself and God. ' I feel wonderfully lone. God knows
I long to be satisfied with His presence.' To his Journal he
committed all his hesitations, doubts and regrets, resolutions
and efforts, his growing life of piety, his attraction to or rejection of the world. There one finds the history of a soul which
does not know whether it can liberate itself or, once having
recognized the hand of God, submit albeit in anguish. ' I am
pierced by anxious thoughts. God knows what my desires
have been and are, and why they are crossed. How did I
strive to find His will to be as my will, and to make a way of
escape from His hand upon me. But a fear has held me, so
that I dare not go on ' (December 15).

He wrote this the day after he had won his greatest victory
over himself, his ambitions and desires, knowing what it had
cost him to ' take the side of clear duty ' and that the battle
was not finished. Samuel Wilberforce had been appointed
Bishop of Oxford, and the Archbishop of York, Chaplain to
the Queen, offered to Manning the post of Sub-Almoner that
his brother-in-law had vacated. In other circumstances
Manning would have been overjoyed at the magnificent
possibilities of the offer, nominal duties, considerable emoluments, influence at Court, followed by a certain bishopric.
But he was afraid—this was the temptation of the world at the
very moment when he had decided to fly from it. He spent a
week in weighing the pros and cons, prayed, took the advice
of others and finally refused. He explained his decision to his
mother in a letter on December 9: ' It would require me to be
absent from my duties here (at Lavington) from Maundy
Thursday to Easter Monday, the most sacred days of the

year—and also on Whit-Sunday. Now I am bound to my
Flock to be with them, unless inevitably hindered, or called
away by a higher spiritual duty. This is not a higher, nor an
equal spiritual duty. Nor is it inevitable, for it would be a
voluntary act on my part to undertake the office. I have
therefore felt that I ought to decline it.' In his Journal he
noted his real personal reasons for refusing:

> I have *prayed* against 'pride, vanity, envy, jealousy,
> rivalry, ambition,' but have done nothing to attain humility.
> I would fain simply deny myself as an offering to Him Who
> pleased not Himself, and perhaps in a distinction and an
> honour having worldly estimation, such a denial is better
> for me than in money or the like. I would fain cross my
> inclinations.

This did not satisfy him and he examined his conscience
further to see whether in his mortification there was any
admixture of pride and self-esteem:

> In the region of counsels, self-chastisement, humiliation,
> self-discipline, penance, and of the Cross, I think I have
> done right. Yet great humility alone can keep me from
> being robbed of all this. To learn to say no, to disappoint
> myself, to choose the harder side, to deny my inclinations,
> to prefer to be less thought of, and to have fewer gifts of the
> world. This is no mistake, and is most like the Cross.
> Only with humility, God grant it to me (Feast of St Paul).

Thus does a soul prepare itself for the grace of divine
illumination.

Nevertheless in May 1846 when his sister-in-law Sophie
Ryder, her husband George and their family joined the
Catholic Church he was greatly distressed and disturbed in
his soul: 'It seems incredible. . . . It is more like death
than anything else. What does He mean us to learn by it?'
The first serious doubts begin to appear in his Journal:

> I am conscious to myself of an extensively changed feeling
> towards the Church of Rome. It seems to me nearer to the
> truth, and the Church of England in greater peril. Our
> divisions seem to me to be fatal as a token, and as a disease.
> . . . I am conscious to be less and less able to preach
> dogmatically. . . . Though not Roman, I cease to be
> Anglican.

In his great need he turned more and more to prayer, and his notes are filled with cries of despair: 'O Spirit of the Fathers and the Saints—come to me—abide with me—dwell in me—enlighten me. . . . Create in me a clean heart.' He notes, almost with relief, that his prayers are heard and he is given new graces which at times leave him completely at a loss.

Strange thoughts have visited me: I have felt that the Episcopate of the English Church is secularised and bound down beyond hope—that there is no κοίναι ἔννοιαι to which to appeal for its restoration. . . . I feel as if a light had fallen on me. My feeling about the Roman Church is not intellectual. I have intellectual difficulties, but the great moral difficulties seem melting—Something keeps rising and saying ' You will end in the Roman Church.'

The thought that has been growing on me, and justifying the Roman doctrine, is the ' new creation.' All seem to hang on this—(1) The Incarnation: (2) The Real Presence, i, Regeneration: ii, Eucharist: (3) the Exaltation of S.M. and Saints. Right or wrong, this family of doctrines is preserved by Rome, and cut or regulated by Protestantism. And I see that the *regula fidei* is held by those who hold them, and least by those who have lost them.

Is all this listening to the tempter?

I do not feel that I should doubt a moment if the choice lay between Rome and any Protestant body. It is only because the English Church seems to me to be distinct from all Protestant bodies that I have any doubt. If the Church of England were away there is nothing in Rome that would repel me with sufficient repulsion to keep me separate, and there is nothing in Protestantism that would attract me. Is the English Church enough to alter the whole case?

Yet I am conscious that I am further from the English Church and nearer Rome than I ever was—How do I know where I may be two years hence? Where was Newman five years ago?

Yet I have no positive doubts about the Church of England. I have difficulties—But the chief thing is the *drawing* of Rome. It satisfies the WHOLE of my intellect, sympathy, sentiment, and nature, in a way proper, and solely belonging to itself. The English Church is an approximate. . . .

This was a terrible judgement on his own Church. His faith was now no more than a feeble flame that a breath might extinguish. It was more fidelity than real faith. Even more characteristic was his admission of the strong attraction of Rome—he was caught in the net of the Fisherman and felt himself torn away from all that he had loved hitherto:

> The meshes are closing round me. I feel less able to say that Rome is wrong—Less able to retain our own—Less able to regain confidence to myself—I feel as if I had shaken the confidence of my people—and I am unable to restore it by any anti-Roman declarations. It is probable that my parish may be troubled. Perhaps He sees that I am settling on my lees—My parish which has steadily risen till now—Perhaps it may go back.
> I feel sad and heavy, tongue-tied and worsted.

Everything seemed to him new and strange. He was detached from the world and his desires and ambitions had disappeared just when they were about to be fulfilled. 'Your kind words,' he wrote to Dodsworth, 'are more soothing to me than anything the newspapers may be—unknown to me—conferring upon me. I somehow feel strangely dead to everything of the sort, and know nothing that says what I mean as well as "henceforth let no man trouble me."' But at other times he felt how strong were the bonds that held him. Thus he noted after a Visitation: 'I was surprised to see with what kindly feeling things went off. I never remember to have been met as this year. And yet I should have expected distance and distrust. All this holds me. Certainly if the actual has a hold on any one it has on me.' At other times he felt he had slipped back, like on the occasion of his stormy meeting with Mrs Lockhart. She had joined her son in the Catholic Church, and demanded from Manning the release of her daughter, who had taken the veil in the first convent of Anglican nuns to be founded. She asked him: 'Mr Archdeacon. Are you sure of the validity of Anglican orders?' In a state of high indignation he demanded: 'Am I sure of the existence of God?' and could not help adding: 'You're a great deal like your dear son!' Of himself at this time he had noted: 'All difficulties as to the sacraments, Purgatory, the Communion of Saints have disappeared. But . . . I believed that though the Church of England had been rent from organic unity and grievously mutilated, nevertheless it survived in its Succession and Pastoral Office.' This explains his attitude of unbreakable fidelity to a Church which he refused to believe was either in schism or heresy. ' The rule that it is a sin to forsake the Church of England if it be not a sin to abide in it, appears to be the turning point of our probation.'

But he could not rest easy, 'in a peace which would be like that of death,' and had to continue his search for a definitive solution to his problems. Now it seemed that God did not wish him to wait longer. So much anxiety had taken its toll of his body. He was staying with his mother at Reigate when he noticed the same symptoms which had marked the onset of his wife's illness ten years earlier. ' Reigate, February 7, 1847—I have just perceived a faint thread of blood probably from the membrane of the throat. My first words were: So be it. *Fiat voluntas tua*, as I remember saying on that day.' He asked himself what he should do if it was a mortal illness: ' What shall I do? First send to (τῷ θεῷ χάρις—March 18) [the name which he omits is that of Laprimaudaye, his curate and his ' confessor in the Church of England': the date is that of his general confession], and make a full confession.— Next, to try to make restitution by acknowledgement, counsel, warning.—Next begin to repent and pray.'

For twelve long weeks he was completely in the hands of God, between life and death, with alternating periods of hope and despair. He meditated, read when he could, wrote in his Journal, examined scrupulously his conscience, mind and heart. His whole life passed before his eyes: all the stages of grace and of conversion ('The growing up of hope, 1845— My illness, 1847'), all his intellectual problems, his moral difficulties, his doubts and his reasons for hope. Above all he arrived at a complete detachment. At last he began to get better and was able to note on May 11: ' Today I went out once more into the free air and sun of heaven.' But Death had merely made an exchange, for the next day, the Eve of the Ascension, his mother died.

His illness was the most important step forward he had made so far, for he emerged from it purified: ' I can say from my soul that I have no longer any desire for wealth, rank, power, name, earthly home, or happiness. . . . That I feel lonely at this time, utterly and unutterably lonely, is most true. But I am willing to be made empty and void if He will come and dwell in me.' He is now close to the solution of his great problem:

> For some time past I have been conscious of one thought enlarging itself in my mind, and one feeling expanding in my heart: that thought has been the reality of the Roman and negatively the unreality of the English Church: that feeling has been a longing for rest in the Church of Rome, and a cessation of rest in the Church of England.

He still hesitates, because he fears that he may be at the mercy of an illusion. 'Am I deceived or deceiving myself? . . . I am horrible afraid. . . . To whom shall I turn? . . . All I can do is to pray. Intellectually I seem to have diminishing doubts. But I am afraid of my own heart.' Later, in autobiographical notes, he explained the development of his thought, and how his doubts were slowly dissipated:

> During that long illness I read S. Leo through—and much of S. Gregory, S. Aug. and S. Optatus. All brought me in greater doubt as to the tenableness of 'moral unity.' It showed me the nature of the Primacy of S. Peter. And at the same time I wrote the IVth Vol. of Sermons which was published the year after. . . . In that volume for the first time I began to find and to express the truth which afterwards brought me to the Church: and has filled my mind with increasing light to this day: I mean the Personal coming, abiding and office of the Holy Ghost. . . .
>
> I had seen human certainty rising up to the summit of intellectual discernment and the *communis sensus* of mankind, but here it could rise no higher. The coming of the Holy Ghost from above to rest upon the intellect of the Church and to elevate it to a supernatural consciousness of faith was the first sight I got of the Infallibility of the Church. It was suggested to me by Melchior Canus' '*Loci Theol.*'
>
> But I profoundly mistrusted myself . . . I was afraid of following what seemed to be a theory of my own. . . . In this state of self-mistrust and fear of going wrong, I went abroad.

He left England at the beginning of July 1847 and travelled through Belgium, Germany and France, and intended to make his way to Italy, and to stay in Rome till the following summer. However, he caught a cold on Lake Lucerne and had to go to bed. In a panic he thought that he might die away from his friends and so returned to London as quickly as he could. It was a false alarm, and he left England again on October 15, this time with his sister Mrs Austen and her husband. They stayed for three weeks at Nice, but his Journal has not a word about his health, nothing about current affairs, a few notes on what he has seen as a tourist. He was completely absorbed in his one over-riding interest: he was impatient to penetrate into the secrets of Catholic faith and piety. Already he had introduced himself to the religious life and spent long hours in conversation with the Capuchins, a prelude to the pilgrimage he was to make to churches and monasteries in Italy.

He arrived in Rome on November 28 and, as soon as he settled in, went to Santa Croce to see Newman. Newman wrote to Henry Wilberforce that he scarcely recognized him because of his illness. Manning did not make any note of their conversation except that 'he told me he was waiting for the Bull of the Hierarchy.' However, Newman left Rome on December 6, while Manning stayed on till May 11. He met many people, some of them old friends like Sidney Herbert, others from Italy and France were quite new, like Padre Ventura and the Abbé Gerbet. Rome interested him enormously because for the first time he saw it as the centre and source of the life of the Church, and because he was a witness of events which affected Rome and the whole of the Peninsula. He was not content, as in 1838, with going to hear sermons, but went to ceremonies and had them explained to him in detail. He did not have the same leisure for long meditations as he had during his illness, but he notes the rapid evolution of his convictions, or his progressive adaptation to life in a really Catholic climate. At Christmas he wrote to Robert Wilberforce: ' Things seem to me clearer, plainer . . . more harmonious: things which were only in the head have got down into the heart.' He was even more explicit in writing to Dodsworth: ' Don't tell any soul what I add now. The sacred beauty with which things are done here is beyond all places. And certainly if the exterior of worship can exhibit the beauty of Holiness it is to be seen in the Pope's

Chapel, and St Peter's, and even in the Parish Churches of
Rome. I say this freely to you, because you and I feel alike
that there are things of no weight in the scale of conscience.'
So he was the better able to judge the poverty of his own
Church, and the new crises which rent it deprived him of the
last means of defending it.

The morning of his departure he was received in audience
by Pius IX. (Oddly enough the *biglietto* was addressed:
al Sig<u>re</u> Arcidiacono Manning.) A long time afterwards he
wrote of this meeting:

> Pius IX talked to me about myself, and England, and
> the Church of England. . . . He then lifted his hands and
> eyes upwards and said: ' The English do many good works,
> and when men do good God gives grace: and my poor
> prayers are offered day by day for England.' I remember
> the pain I felt at seeing how unknown we (the Anglicans)
> were to the Vicar of Jesus Christ. It made me feel our
> isolation. Before that audience I had seen him passing in
> his carriage through the Piazza di Spagna. I knelt down
> on the ground.

Manning was in no haste to go back to England, and spent five
weeks on the journey, because he wanted to see ' Lombardy
in the first days of its freedom.' Actually he does not seem to
have been greatly interested in the Revolution, but rather
wanted to be a simple pilgrim in the country of St Francis of
Assisi. Here too he came to learn about St Charles Borromeo.
It was the end of his spiritual initiation. Every day he went
to Mass either in a monastery or a church, and every evening
Benediction had a special attraction for him, because he said
that it revealed the Incarnation to him. The first note in his
Journal at Nice was dated: ' 4th November—Feast of S. Charles
Borromeo.' His last note in Italy was written in Milan after
visiting the tomb of the Saint.

> In Milan happened what I always have felt like a call
> from St Charles. . . . After seeing the shrine below, I
> went up and knelt looking down upon his body through the
> Confession. The High Mass was going on. I was thinking
> in prayer, ' if only I could know that St Charles who
> represents the Council of Trent was right and we wrong.'

c

The Deacon was singing the Gospel and the last words, *et erit unum ovile et unus pastor*, came upon me as if I had never heard them before.

It seemed like an answer to his prayer: the voice of St Charles calling him unequivocally to enter the one fold. Manning was touched, and converted in his heart. He was to go back to England with the sad decision to lead Anglicanism to its only logical conclusion. But his heart was heavy with apprehension and anguish at the thought that if he did not leave his Church, it would leave him.

On his return he was faced with a new situation, 'the miserable, even thrice miserable, Hampden affair.' Dr Hampden, whose doctrine had been censured by the University, had now been nominated by Lord John Russell to the see of Hereford. This happened while Manning was in Rome, and he wrote at the time in terms somewhat similar to those that Newman had used to him in 1843:

> I feel my position altered by the event, and unless the reasons which I will give can be shown to be without force, I am afraid of thinking of the future—I am convinced that Hampden's Bampton Lectures are heretical in *matter*— And still more, that they are heretical in *form*. . . . The Episcopate is fully made partaker in his heterodoxy by his consecration, and the whole Church, priesthood, and laity in communion with the Episcopate. . . . The separation of the English episcopate from the whole episcopate under heaven, the denial of Catholic doctrine in *substance* by a large body of the English priesthood, e.g. the doctrine of the Sacraments etc. . . . The rejection of Catholic doctrine in *form* by the rejection of Catholic tradition as the rule of faith, the historical fact that the Church of England has made common cause with Protestantism as a mass as in the Jerusalem Bishopric; all these have for a long time deprived me of the power of claiming for it the un-doubted guidance of the Holy Spirit along the path of Catholic tradition. It is not from the Church we receive it, but from our own books and our own private judgement.
>
> I am left without defence. . . . And this event has brought out a miserable truth, namely that the civil power is the ultimate judge of doctrine in England, a principle which is not more heretical than atheistical.

In spite of himself, he has to draw the inevitable conclusion:

My dear Robert, you will not misunderstand me, as if I thought myself to be anything. God knows what I am humbles and alarms me. And it is under this condition that I add, that I do not know how I can serve a body I cannot defend. I seem *reduced* to a choice between my faith and all its foundations on one side, and all that life has, which is dear to me, on the other. The grounds on which I have striven to keep others in the Church of England are falsified. And I dare not seek or retain any influence but that of Truth, and the influence over individuals which only Truth has given henceforward has no foundation.

He ends with a protestation, strangely similar to the one which Newman had made some time earlier:

Dear Robert, do not think I am under any effect of ill-health, or sensitiveness, or locality, or momentary provocation, or the like. What I have written has been steadily advancing in my mind these ten years, and outward events do but verify old fears, and project old convictions upon realities.

He was at Genoa when he learned that, in spite of all legal opposition, the nomination of Hampden had been confirmed, and he wrote: ' That evening I was in the Croce di Matta looking over the port and the shipping, as the sun was going down in its glory. The English paper was brought to me announcing Hampden's confirmation. I felt that it was the beginning of the end.'

Back in England, he consulted his friends, Robert Wilberforce, Gladstone and Dodsworth. His position was clear: if he could no longer defend the Church of England, he could no longer serve it. And yet—he still wanted to believe in it. He could not bring himself not to believe that the English Church (not the Establishment) was ' a living portion of the Church of Christ.' Because of this he still waited. But he felt it necessary to discharge his own responsibility by explaining his position. He did this in a Charge addressed to his clergy in which he went straight to the point:

The Right Reverend person of whom we speak declared his acceptance of the whole doctrine of Faith: he was consecrated not upon the confession of his theological works, but on publication of subscription to the Catholic creeds. Of the fact of subscription the fact of consecration is our pledge: of sincerity who can conceive a doubt? For these reasons it appears that we are now released from the necessity of forming opinions as to past theological statements justly censured.

This legal argument was the strict minimum that allowed him to wait: ' If I had failed to find a just defence,' he wrote to Dodsworth, ' I am afraid to think of what must have followed.' It satisfied Dodsworth, although he did remark: ' What you say is literally and legally true, but scarcely includes the whole *moral* view of the matter. A murderer or pickpocket may escape through defect or maladministration of the law.' Nevertheless a weight was lifted from Manning's mind, at least because he had gained a respite: ' I have had things to cheer me,' he confides to a friend, ' great depth and devotion in individuals with no tinge of Anglicanism or any such sham.' He absorbed himself in the direction of souls, in theological discussions with Robert Wilberforce, and in many different works, among them the important problem of education which he made the subject of his Charge in 1849.

Aubrey de Vere went to see him at Lavington during the autumn and has left us an impressive picture: ' He is the most venerable, the most refined, the most gentle, the most spiritual and earnest man I know.' He tells of long walks through the woods right up to the Downs, with Manning holding forth on theology and poetry, and, in the evening, strolling in the garden of the Rectory, quoting passages from Dante's *Paradiso*: ' There is no poetry like Dante's: it is S. Thomas Aquinas put into verse! These two men were the greatest of human minds ! '

These were the last moments of rest and the last time he was to enjoy the delights of Lavington. The anxious questioning began once again, and was more anguished for others, such as Allies, his sister-in-law Mary and his brother-in-law Henry Wilberforce. The last-named had pressing letters from Newman: ' I have heard something about you this morning which makes me say " Send for me, and I will come to you at once—by return of post." Do not let anything stand between conviction and its legitimate consequence.' And two days later: 'I can't help writing. How can you delay? Oh my dearest H.W., may not this be a crisis in your eternal destiny.' But Manning who had led Mary to the threshold of the Catholic Church now begged her to wait, and to make Henry wait with her, for a little while longer. We can guess from his letter what has happened:

(1st Sunday of Advent). . . Henry is so near and so dear to me that what he says and does is almost my own. . . . I therefore do not know whether to be sorry or glad at what has happened. I have intentionally spared you the perplexity of what I was bearing myself. I did so because I felt that until I could have a moral conviction that I am not misleading myself I could not be sure that I was not misleading others, and you among them.

I read you that Sermon because I intended to put it out as a statement of my belief. And my purpose is, by the will of God, to publish as full a book on the subject of Infallibility as I have light to make. And by that book to take my path.

I have said this to you because I have taken the responsibility of your guidance until now. I do not shrink from saying that intellectual convictions are, I think, not enough taken alone. . . . With your moral shrinking I do not think you are called to any step 'without delay.' . . . You remember my promise that the day I feel my soul to demand anything for its safety, you shall know. I have not forgotten it. . . . On St Andrew's Day at the altar what you ask of me was my one prayer, and I offered myself as I have done again and again—as I told you before and never so often as in Rome—to follow on the spot, if only I can have not sign or token but the conviction of a moral agent that it is the will of my Lord.

Whether this will give you cause still to hold by the hand which has never consciously led you astray—but has even when you were at ease broken your peace to lead you where God led him, I leave to the inspiration of His grace. . . . Pray for me sevenfold—for to mistake in such a path as this is to one who must give account of souls, something like death.

Little can be added to that letter which shows so clearly the drama which was nearing its climax. Three days later the appeal of Gorham to the Privy Council was heard. The Bishop of Exeter had refused to allow the Rev. J. C. Gorham to take a living in his diocese because he did not accept the doctrine of baptismal regeneration. Gorham appealed first to the Court of Arches and his appeal was now before the Judicial Committee of the Privy Council. It was made up of seven laymen, with the Archbishops of York and Canterbury and the Bishop of London as assessors. The very principle of a civil (and political) body being the supreme court of appeal for spiritual affairs disturbed Manning greatly. The fact that a civil body should be called on to decide an essential point of dogma seemed to him to bring in question the very nature of the Church as well as the principle of the Royal Supremacy. The letters that he wrote to his friends, W. Dodsworth, Robert Wilberforce, Gladstone, J. R. Hope, and two lawyers, Sir John Dodson and Baron Alderson, left no possibility of ambiguity: 'The pending appeal is a violation of the Divine Office of the Church in respect to its doctrine—I say *the appeal*, because it is indifferent which way the judgement may go.' Consequently he said he was ' unable to obey the existing law,' and he wondered how he could still ' with a just conscience towards God, hold offices of which that oath of submission to the existing Ecclesiastical Law is a condition.'

For Dodsworth the appeal did not change anything and did not constitute ' *of itself* a sufficient ground for immediate secession.' But he thought some action was called for and suggested a meeting of their friends: 'I wish we may be able to go *in concert*. This is the object of our proposed meeting, and we can afterwards call in others. Nothing will justify us in going, save the conviction that it is to save our souls.' However Manning insisted:

Reconsider the case in this form. If the principle of the Royal Supremacy subjects doctrine to the final judgement of the Civil Power it is a duty to our Lord to refuse the Supremacy. In this case the necessity of resigning our office held upon *oath* is complete. But I am willing to try to move heaven and earth to cure the evil—and so destroy the necessity. But if in this we fail the case is imperative for resignation. I have said nothing of secession—though to resign in the E.C. is in fact to submit to the R. I will do anything with you to break up the necessity—before moving a foot.

He had said the same to Robert Wilberforce in another way: ' How can a priest twice judged unfit for cure of souls by the Church, be put in charge of souls at the sentence of the Civil Power without overthrowing the divine office of the Church?' Wilberforce begged him to wait for the decision of the Committee and said: ' I see not why you should act now any more than at any period since 1845.' J. R. Hope expressed the same view, but the greatest evil, he said, was that the Gorham Appeal had revealed a situation which had existed since the Reformation. He added he could find no theory to justify the isolated position of the Church of England in relation to the rest of the Church, still less for its subjection to the civil power. If the Royal Supremacy is wrong, it had been so from the beginning. The Gorham Appeal was no different from previous appeals except for the matter which it involved, and on this subject he said: ' If a false judgement must be pronounced . . . whatever the mouthpiece which utters the judgement, if the Church does not repudiate it, there is an article of the Creed struck out and then indeed there will be a weight thrown into the scale against our allegiance.'

On March 8, 1850, the Judicial Committee of the Privy Council reversed the judgement of the Court of Arches and awarded the decision to the heretic Gorham as against Bishop Philpotts. Of the seven lay judges only one, Vice-Chancellor Knight Bruce, and of the Bishops only one, the Bishop of London, voted against Gorham. The Archbishops of Canterbury and York voted for him.

Naturally there were considerable repercussions and Manning, after several days of discussion in London, left for Lavington leaving J. R. Hope to attend meetings and speak in his name. He had no wish to join in the negotiations and arguments because he felt that they were merely bargaining with the truth. He could no longer stand the blindness of men of piety like Pusey and Keble, nor the deliberate abstention of a convinced and sincere man like Gladstone. The last meeting of the friends was held at Gladstone's house on March 18 and ended by them drawing up a Declaration of

Protest, signed by Manning, Henry and Robert Wilberforce, Dodsworth, Keble and Pusey for Oxford, Mill for Cambridge, Archdeacon Thorpe of Bristol, Bennett of St Paul's, Knightsbridge, and four lawyers: Hope, Badeley, Cavendish and Talbot. On that day Gladstone had judged it convenient to be absent.

On the following day Manning called a meeting of clergy at Chichester where a similar protest was passed almost unanimously. It looked as though there would be another lull. ' My purpose,' he wrote to Robert Wilberforce, ' is to stay a while and see what others will do, e.g., the Bishops and clergy at large: to affirm and put to the test the principles . . . and if they are rejected to follow them.' And again on May 5 he summed up the reasons ' which make me strive to subdue both haste and fear—it is a fearful conclusion to say that 10 generations in the last 300 years, and among them visibly penitent and holy souls, dwelling in God far more than I, died out of His Church and were deceived.' He then added: ' I need more to decide a question with such tremendous issues for time and for eternity. It would be like one mistake upon a death-bed.'

He waited to see the effect of the action of Bishop Philpotts who, now that his appeal had been rejected, renewed his solemn declaration that ' any archbishop or bishop, or any official of any archbishop or bishop, who shall institute J. C. Gorham within our diocese—whereas the same hath not retracted and disclaimed his heretical doctrines—will thereby incur the sin of supporting and favouring heresy, and we do renounce and repudiate all communion with him, be he whom he may.' But these proved to be empty words without effect, for on August 5 Gorham was installed by the Dean of Arches, acting on the fiat of the Archbishop of Canterbury. The Bishop of London had tried to change the existing legislation and proposed that the Upper Court of Convocation should become the supreme court of appeal for all matters of doctrine. The Lords rejected the proposal by an overwhelming majority, and only four bishops voted for it. The Archbishop of Canterbury abstained.

Manning, on July 2, 1850, published a letter to the Bishop of Chichester entitled *The Appellate Jurisdiction of the Crown in*

Matters Spiritual. He established that : ' 1. The Royal
Supremacy since Henry VIII is not the Royal Supremacy
before. 2. That in the appellate jurisdiction lately exercised:
i. the Divine Office of the Church as the guardian of the
doctrine and the discipline of Christ has been violated—
ii. legal protection has been given to heresy—iii. an offence
inflicted against the whole authority of faith, and Divine
doctrine thrust down to the level of a human opinion.' He
agreed to join in a last effort and to appear at a meeting
organized on July 23 by the London Church Union. He
spoke last, and his mildness contrasted strongly with the
vehemence of the previous speakers, although he insisted on the
gravity of the situation: ' This meeting would do more harm
than good if, after such an exhibition of zeal and earnestness,
a man should go home and think he had done a great act, and
that no more was necessary to be done. May this be averted.'
Nevertheless two days later Archbishop Sumner refused to
accept their protest because he could not ' reverse the sentence
of the legitimate court.' He added: ' Nothing that I find
in the law of God gives me reason to believe that I should be
acting in conformity with His will if I refused Mr. Gorham
admission to the cure of souls on the ground of his hesitancy
to affirm the spiritual regeneration of every baptized child.'

There only remained for Manning to try the supreme test,
an appeal ' to the Church at large.' Robert Wilberforce had
written to him on June 7: ' We ought to give time to see
whether the Clergy are accessible to arguments which shall
state to them the real nature of the question.' But all the
arguments had been proposed and nothing had happened.
The night after the London meeting Manning found a way of
estimating the result:

> I remember. . . . I woke about 4 o'clock, and lay
> awake long. I then worked out the Declaration against
> the Royal Supremacy; admitting it in all civil matters, but
> rejecting it in all spiritual and mixed matters. I then went
> and woke Robert Wilberforce (I was staying at Bp Wilber-
> force's house in Eaton Place) and put it before him. He
> accepted it at once. We then got it into writing and invited
> Dr Mill to sign it with us. We then sent it to every clergy-
> man and layman who had signed the Oath of Supremacy,

and to all colleges and newspapers, inviting signatures. . . .
About 1,800 clergymen signed it out of 20,000, and I saw
the game was up. It was a fair test fully applied, and it
received next to no response.

The months which followed, during the summer of 1850,
were a time of extreme distress and yet of serenity. From all
sides came appeals to Manning, sometimes quite moving, from
his friends who wished to hold him back. But there were
others, among his intimates, who were calling him in the
opposite direction. W. Maskell was received into the
Catholic Church in June, Allies on September 11, and Henry
Wilberforce on the 15th. Mrs Allies and Mary Wilberforce
had already been received. The effect of these repeated blows
is shown in Manning's pathetic letters to Robert Wilberforce,
it is clear that the end is near. ' (September 19, 1850)
The late events have not changed our position, but *revealed* it,
and they who see it are bound to submit themselves to the
universal Church . . . My dear Robert, I feel as if my time
were drawing near, and that, like death, it will be, if it must be,
alone. But I shrink with all the love and fear of my soul.
Pray for me.' Robert Wilberforce replied with a wild letter:
he was not ready himself, and if Manning did not at least wait
to see the results of their enquiry, what would people say?
Manning replied on September 26: ' I have no thought of a
hasty step. . . . If I know that I should die this day six
months I should speak as if life were over and death near. . . .
The state of my mind is a settled conviction that it must end
in only one way.'

Gladstone is going abroad for the winter and invites Manning
to go with him. The thought comes to him: why not go and
so have time ' for last reflections and dying thoughts '? So he
asks in a letter of October 4: ' Give me now your kind advice.
Can I go without resigning? Does not public honour require
it? Resigning does not compel going further. But can I hold
office of trust and emoluments without clashing with up-
rightness?' And again on October 22:

I am not afraid of seeming to fly from a storm. . . . The
true and overruling reason is that I am so deeply convinced
that the Church is infallible through the guidance of the
Holy Spirit, and that the Church of England is not under

that guidance, as to leave me day by day less choice. . . .
I believe it is a revelation of a position untenable ab initio.
. . . We are in material heresy and that throws light on
our separation, and I believe we are in schism.

But the bonds that hold him are so strong that he suffers the
wrench in his soul: ' I am full of dread lest the truth of
conscience should be lost by waiting and listening to the
suggestions of flesh and blood.'

But God once again, in His Providence, came to his aid.
A new storm arose, in which he was to find the unanimity he
had sought in vain—but it was against the Catholic Church
and not for it. And so at last Manning found himself outside
the Church of England. After the restoration of the Hierarchy
by a Papal Brief of September 29, 1850, Wiseman, now
Cardinal Archbishop of Westminster, had written his famous
Pastoral Letter of October 7, ' From out of the Flaminian
Gate.' The immediate result was an outburst of feeling
against what was labelled ' Papal aggression.' Meetings of
protest were organized throughout the country by clergy and
laity, and the Prime Minister, Lord John Russell, wrote a
letter to Bishop Maltby of Durham which almost seemed to
incite the people to mob violence. For Manning it marked
the definite failure of his Church. Many sincere souls that
he thought he had nearly won over were pulled back by the
collective wave of passion that swept the country. He was
asked by his clergy to call a general meeting at which they
could register their protest against the act of papal aggression.
The Bishop of Chichester wrote to him to say that he had
refused to join his name to the demand, and that he deplored it.
But Manning called the meeting, for, he said, ' this constitutes
a *peremptory* cause.'

On November 15 he wrote to Robert Wilberforce to say
that he had seen his bishop and had told him ' that he was
convinced of the unlawfulness by Christ's law of the Royal
Supremacy—that he believed it to be the instrument which
had severed the Church of England from the Church Universal
—that the act of the Pope was the legitimate consequence he
could not oppose—that he knew the views of the clergy to be
different and could not share in their proceedings.' So he
asked ' either to resign at once—or to call the meeting

ministerially and state his dissent and resignation.' The
bishop expressed the wish that he should call the meeting but
reconsider his resignation.

> I feel that my foot is in the river [he wrote to Robert
> Wilberforce]. It is cold and my heart is sad. But where
> faith can act, I seem to feel that the world has subdued the
> Church of England to itself, and that the kingdom of our
> Lord is not from hence. I do not say one word to urge you,
> dearest Robert, God forbid: I know your heart is as mine,
> and I have gone through your present state. Only do
> nothing against what may be found at last to be the Will
> and Presence of our Lord.

The meeting of the clergy of Chichester took place on
Friday, November 22, in the library of the cathedral, now
restored as the Lady Chapel. Manning made no contribution
whatsoever to the proceedings, but at the end he replied to
the vote of thanks:

> I said that ' it was the first and only time in ten years in
> which I had been separated in conviction and action from
> them: that I had no choice ': that ' necessity was laid upon
> me ': that ' I thanked them with all my heart for their
> brotherly love and the many acts of kindness and friendship,
> private and public, in the ten years I had held office among
> them ': that ' I should never forget it or them.' My dear
> old friend the Dean was crying, and many others. So we
> ended and parted. It was our last meeting, and the end of
> my work in the Church of England.

They all knew that he was leaving them for ever. On
Tuesday, November 26, he was present at the consecration of
the new church of St Mary Magdalen which his curate
Laprimaudaye had built at West Lavington at the extreme
end of the parish in the direction of Midhurst. Samuel
Wilberforce preached, and Robert was there, having come
specially because Samuel had said: ' I hardly dare hope to
have Manning again with us.' He had celebrated for the last
time on Sunday, December 1, but had said nothing to his
parishioners:' . . . a heaviness of soul such as I hardly dare
speak of love, tenderness, long and fond memories of home and
flock were around me and upon me. But through all a calm
clear conviction stood unmoved.' The following Tuesday,

December 3, he left for London. He went to Cadogan Place, to stay as usual with his sister Mrs Carey, but no longer wore the ' emblems of his office.' One of his penitents met him in the street and seeing him dressed thus was completely overcome, because she was now sure that ' it was all over.' He wrote to Gladstone to say that he had given up all thought of joining him, as he wanted to be in the midst of his friends ' to whom I wish to give all evidence I can of the calmness and deliberation with which I have acted and hope to act in this time of trial.' Faithful to his promise to ' do nothing without warning him,' he had written to Hope on November 22. They confirmed their decision ' to keep together,' and were completely agreed that ' it is either Rome or licence of thought and will.'

Others of his friends were received into the Catholic Church in the course of December: Laprimaudaye, his curate and ' confessor in the Church of England,' Mr Sergeant Bellasis and William Dodsworth. To Gladstone, who had written anxiously, he replied: ' I will do nothing till I have seen you.' On the other hand, he wrote to Laprimaudaye:

> I may say to you, and you alone, that I cannot think to be long as I am now. I have been dealing one by one with the many bonds of duty which bind me on every side, unravelling some and breaking others. I owe still some acts of deliberation to particular persons. When they are discharged I shall believe that I stand before God all alone, with no responsibility but for my own soul. And then I trust I shall not be wanting to the inspirations of His will. Pray for me, dearest friend, I have been suffering deeply. But God's will be done.

He did not take his obligations and responsibilities lightly, and they weighed heavy upon him. He gave himself three months in which to set forth the motives for his actions and to test the truth of his convictions. He lived a retired life and for the morning and evening services of Lavington had substituted the recitation of the Breviary. He wrote to Miss Maurice: ' It takes from 2 to $2\frac{1}{2}$ hours every day, and being said at fixed times supports the regularity of my day.' On Sunday mornings he went to the early Communion at St Paul's, Knightsbridge, the parish from which Bennett had resigned in December. But soon he was to write: ' I feel as if I can do this no more. It is a thing too sacred to be approached without undoubting faith. And this in the Church of England I have not.' On March 17 he wrote to the same correspondent:

> Now I will say that I feel this time of waiting to be near its end. I have been praying that some restraining grace may intervene if it be not the will of God for me to go forward. If no such restraint interposes I think that the week between Passion Sunday and Palm Sunday will close my long tarrying before the Gate.

He had taken this decision with J. R. Hope, with whom he had reviewed ' the whole ground again ' so that they could be sure that they had made no mistakes and that their conclusions were correct. In the same month of March he had by an official act made final his double resignation as archdeacon of Chichester and Rector of Lavington. He tells of how he won this last victory and thanked Our Lady for it:

> I remember the immense sorrow that came over me—not that my reason or my will wavered for a moment. I started from Cadogan Place to go to Badeley in the Temple. But when I got to Apsley House I said to myself ' This is going to human consolation ' and I turned back. It did me good for after that I do not think I have sought consolation from human sources. In a few days I went into the City and executed my legal resignation of office and benefice before Notary Public. Then I came back and went over Blackfriars Bridge to St George's, Southwark, to the chapel of the Blessed Sacrament: and then and there I said my first ' Hail Mary,' for so long as I was under subscription I never used an invocation. I was then a free man. *Laqueus contritus est et nos liberati sumus.*

He took leave one by one of all his friends. To the Rev W. Ayling, who had been charged by the Rural Chapter of Lavington to draw up an address ' expressing as much as words could express their pain and grief,' he wrote: ' I can only say that I shall always look back upon the intercourse I have been permitted to have with you as the greatest blessing of my life—I will not attempt to say more—feelings sometimes are too deep for words.'

Manning was at last free to accomplish what he had called

' my last act of reason and my first act of faith ' by submitting to Rome. One last trial awaited him: he could not believe that he was not a priest, and could not enter as a priest into the Roman communion. He spent five hours with a theologian in hot discussion on the validity of Anglican Orders, in which he believed ' with a consciousness stronger than all reasoning.' In the end, he made a supreme act of humility and accepted what was the heaviest of all sacrifices.

On Friday, April 4, 1851, he moved from Cadogan Place to Hope's place at 14 Queen Street, Mayfair. The following morning they made their decision. A few moment's walk and they were in Hill Street and so at Farm Street. Father Brownbill received them and made appointments for the morrow. Manning was to be received in the morning before High Mass, Hope in the afternoon. He could not but rejoice with them, but left them under no illusions. ' His manner,' writes Lady Georgiana Fullerton, ' was enough to teach them that they could bring to the Church nothing and were to receive from her everything.' Manning submitted joyfully and as they came out into the street he said to Hope, ' Now my career is ended.'

Manning described the reception to Miss Maurice; ' It was all most private, from $9\frac{1}{2}$ to $10\frac{1}{2}$ . . . I had a special desire to fix it on Passion Sunday . . . The process was Confession, Conditional Baptism, Profession of Faith, made by my desire, and Absolution. Then I went to the High Mass, which to me even when outside has been the divinest act of worship upon earth.' Hope was received at three in the afternoon. ' How blessed an end!' Manning wrote to him a little later, ' as the soul said to Dante " *E de martirio venni a questa pace.*" ' He presented him with one of his most cherished books, the *Paradisus Animae*, with the inscription ' In memory of Passion Sunday and its gift of grace to me.' Hope in return gave him a copy of the *Speculum Vitae Sacerdotalis*, and inscribed it ' *Stantes erant pedes nostri.*'

There we may leave them—in peace and in light—for such a story has no need of an epilogue. Manning wrote later: ' An sense of wonder had arisen how we could so long have failed to perceive a truth now self-evident. All I can say is, " One thing I know, that whereas I was blind, now I see." '

II

MANNING AND HIS OBLATES

By DENIS WARD, o.s.c.

THE Catholics of England had scarcely begun to breathe freely, following the Act of Emancipation, when they had their breath taken away from them by the lightning tactics of Nicholas Wiseman who, whether as President of Oscott, Vicar Apostolic of the London District, or Cardinal Archbishop of Westminster and first Metropolitan of the restored hierarchy, had but one objective, viz., the conversion of England. Not that he expected this to be achieved within the span of his own life as one of his earliest inspirers, George Spencer, would have had him believe possible, but he was determined that no effort on his part should be spared and every encouragement be given to those who would labour with him for the early return of England to her ancient Faith.

But this enthusiasm met with little response among the old Catholics who felt that the flamboyant zeal of the Roman Prelate and what they regarded as the equivocations and insincerities of the Tractarian Movement would rouse the fury of the English people, with the result that the Church might be driven back into the catacombs from which it had just emerged. Nor was the *Romanità* of this would-be Augustine much to their liking. He was above all else a Roman of the Romans, conscious of his high dignity even though he might be, as he himself once put it, a Prince of the Church ' whose Court consisted of one priest.' Moreover, he had pledged himself to make the Church known ' as she is in the fulness of her growth, with the grandeur of her ritual, the beauty of her devotions, the variety of her institutions '; a far cry from the unobtrusive Catholicity of England and little to its taste. And when to the Roman was added an Ambrosian flavour, in the appointing of a convert layman to teach theology to the future priests of Westminster and the ordaining of an Anglican clergyman within weeks of his reception into the

Church and without any of the training which precedes the conferring of Holy Orders, then the Catholics of England, while they could scarcely doubt that history was being made, could hardly be expected to believe that it was being repeated. But in spite of all misgivings the lay theologian remained the soul of orthodoxy and in the neophyte Wiseman had truly discerned the successor to his Archiepiscopal See.

The announcement in *The Tablet* to the effect that the newly ordained Mr. Manning was proceeding to Rome ' for the commencement of his ecclesiastical studies ' was true if taunting, but Manning had only assented to being ordained within ten weeks of becoming a Catholic on condition that he would be allowed to follow a normal course of theological studies afterwards. And knowing that his Ordination had taken place without the knowledge and sanction of the Holy See, he was by no means certain of the kind of reception he would have on his arrival in Rome. He need not have had any qualms, for he was to find, as so many have found before and since, that around the Seven Hills there still echoes, and by no means faintly, the aphorism of Gregory the Great: ' *Non Angli sed angeli* '—unless proof be given to the contrary.

Shortly after taking lodgings in Via del Tritone he received a visit from Mgr. Hohenloe, a member of the Papal household, who brought the information that the Holy Father wished to see him that evening (December 4, 1851). At that first meeting Pius IX told Manning that he wished him to enter the *Accademia Ecclesiastica*, that celebrated institution in which the future diplomats of the Vatican were trained and which was commonly known as the Nursery of Cardinals. Manning entered the *Accademia* on December 12, 1851, and remained there three years. ' During those three years,' he says, ' I received from Pius IX a fatherly kindness. I saw him nearly every month and he spoke with me fully on many things and gave me freedom to speak with him. It was the beginning of a confidence that was never broken.' Of the many things discussed in these intimate talks Manning mentions only one, but a very significant one in view of later history. ' Another time,' he says, ' I remember standing with him in a window of the Library looking upon Rome and talking of the Temporal Power. I said: Holy Father, there is no choice but the

D

Vatican or the Catacombs. He said: It is no question of the extent of territory or provinces, but the Pontiff must be in a territory, however small, of his own.'

As to his fitness to exercise the Sacred Orders so recently bestowed, that was quickly decided by the conferring of the Faculties of Missionary Apostolic. Soon afterwards came an offer, through Mgr. Talbot, of the post of Privy Chamberlain, but this he refused as likely to hinder his work in England. It is events such as these at the very beginning of his Catholic life which make nonsense of the accusations made later, that he was a seeker after places and ambitious for power. What need had he to seek when so much was freely given? It would be as logical to regard the privileges bestowed by Pius IX on one who as yet had done nothing to merit them, as so much bribery. (Lytton Strachey, of course, maintained that this was the case.) Three years before his conversion Manning had an audience with Pius IX of which he gave a simple and straightforward account, mentioning the Pope's great kindness and his interest in England and English affairs. For Strachey this becomes a ' mysterious interview ' at which he finds it ' easy to imagine ' that Pius IX, in his seductive Italian voice, gave what amounted to an A Cappella version of ' *Deh! vieni, non tardar.* . . . *Ti vo' la fronte incoronar di rose!* ' But then, others imagined that Newman was ordained a Catholic priest before he left the Church of England and that Manning was thrown into prison by the Pope on his arrival in Rome in 1851! What one can more easily imagine is that the English literary recluse owed a good deal of his knowledge of Roman Ecclesiastics and their odd little ways to the pages of Alexandre Dumas, in spite of the omission of that name from his bibliography.

Manning could hardly fail to appreciate the significance of being placed by the Pope at the *Accademia Ecclesiastica*. It could only mean that he was ultimately intended to occupy one of the positions for which that institute was the training school. That he realized this is evident from the fact that, when in 1853 Wiseman asked him to return to England to help him fulfil his long cherished desire of founding a Congregation of Missionary Priests, he referred the matter to Pius IX who said: ' Remain where you are.' In 1854 Wiseman visited

Rome and obtained the Degree of Doctor of Theology for Manning, at the same time asking for his release for work in Westminster. Again Manning went to Pius IX for direction. This time the Pope consented, saying: '*Il povero Cardinale insiste così* that I can no longer refuse him. *Ma per dirla il mio intimo pensiero, io voleva che lei restasse a Roma finchè avrei potuto metterla in qualche posto.*' The Cardinal desired it, the Pope assented; it was sufficient. The place-seeker turned his back on certain honour and preferment to face an uncertain future. And the verdict of Pius IX was: '*È sempre docile.*'

Wiseman's idea of founding a Missionary Congregation was of many years' standing and arose as a result of his memorable tour of England in 1835-36.

What I am most anxious to accomplish [he wrote from Rome when it became certain that his future work lay in England] is to establish a small community of Missioners who, living in a common house, should go ' bini ' from place to place giving lectures, retreats, etc., in different dioceses, so as to be out several months at a time and then repose, so that those at home could be engaged in conducting at certain intervals retreats for laymen or clergy in the house. It would do to begin with six or eight, but they must be truly filled with the spirit of devotion and piety, as well as learned and fluent, not to say eloquent. This idea of mine is well known to the young men here, and I would engage out of my small number to find two or three (two Northerns) who would devote themselves to the work. It only requires someone to lead and show the way, and I am sure others would rise up or come forward.

However, the idea had to be shelved for, though it was warmly approved by Pope Gregory XVI, it found little favour among the English Vicars Apostolic. In Wiseman's view the need still existed and when he came to the London District he tried to meet it by the introduction of various Religious Orders. But he says in writing to Faber:

I am just—for the great work—where I began! Not one of them can—for it cannot be want of will—undertake it. They are prevented by their Rule from helping . . . at least in any but a particular and definite way. . . . I wish all to follow out their Rules but they impress me strongly

with the want of elasticity and power of adaptation in
them. . . . The work which is required cannot be fully
carried out except by a Community. . . . Yet, as it
appears, they [the works he has in mind] are not com-
patible with a Religious Order from want of expansive
power in this. I am driven to seek for a quid medium
between the secular and the religious state; or, as I described it to Mr. Manning, ' an Oratory with external
action,' and I do not think that dear San Filippo will be
angry with me for trying to get it. . . . It has appeared
to me that Providence has now given me the opportunity
of gathering such a band. Mr Manning, I think, under-
stands my wishes and feelings, and is ready to assist me;
several will, I hope, join him, and I hope also some old and
good priests. We shall be able to work together, because
there will be no exemptions from episcopal jurisdiction, and
none of the jealousy on the one side, and the delicacy on
the other of interference or suggestion. I do not see how
the multifarious missionary work I have proposed can be
carried on without frequent communication with the
Bishop.

To the fulfilment of this desire Manning was now to address
his indomitable energy and zeal. But always he maintained
that Wiseman was the true founder of the Oblates, himself
merely the instrument for the carrying out of the work, and
that if any other had been forthcoming he would gladly have
stepped down in his favour. Indeed in one of his letters to
Robert Wilberforce, the dearest friend of his Anglican days,
for whose conversion he had laboured so many years, we find
him urging the latter to come to Rome and join him in the
founding of a Community of Priests with Wilberforce as Head
and himself as subject. But this was not to be; Wilberforce
died of cholera in February 1857, while a student at the
Accademia.

I then came back to England (1854) and the Cardinal
desired me to begin the Congregation of the Oblates of
St Charles [says Manning in his journals]. I was slow
about it but not from unwillingness or disobedience but
from doubt of myself. However, in 1856 I drew up the
first outline of the Rule from St Charles' Milanese Rule.
The Cardinal accepted it and I went in November to

Milan to S. Sepolcro and Rho and learned all I could of the living tradition of the Oblates. I then went on to Rome. As soon as I laid it before Cardinal Barnabo (the Prefect of Propaganda) he said: '*Queste sono le mie idee,*' and from that moment he did all in his power to promote it. He laid it before the Holy Father. In my next audience the Pope said '*senza voti*' which I took for command.

Writing to Wiseman from Rome, Manning draws attention to the following salient points in the Constitution and Rules of the new Congregation:

1. That they should be closely united to the Bishop and should be as it were his familia.

2. That they should have just so much internal constitution as to raise and conserve their spirit and theological standard and corroborate both.

3. That they should be completely mixed among the clergy of the diocese.

> This last point [he says] appears to me to be of the greatest importance, and I have avoided everything which can distinguish them from the rest of the priests, or in any way generate a different spirit, or put on a grave religious character . . . the rules are so drawn that, dropping only so much as gives continuity and form to the congregation, the horarium and mode of life might be adopted by any secular priest or in any missionary rectory.

In February 1857 Wiseman wrote congratulating Manning on the progress that had been made and in the following month he wrote:

> I particularly entreat you that should the Holy Father name you Canon [in place of Dr. Whitty who had joined the Society of Jesus] you will not decline. There are many reasons for it. It will be the first time the Holy Father will have exercised the prerogative of nomination and I wish the precedent to be given. It will be most gratifying to the Chapter. It will be acceptable to every class of Catholics. It will prove that the Oblates are not a distinct Order, but true secular priests. It will give at once a high position to the Institute in the diocese, and stamp it with the strongest seal of approbation both from Rome and here. For everybody will and shall know that I have most fully concurred in the nomination.

Manning was by no means sure, and rightly so, that his appointment to the Westminster Chapter would be as favourably received as Wiseman hoped and his consternation was even greater when the Holy Father nominated him not only Canon but Provost of the Chapter. But he accepted the appointment because of Wiseman's plea and in the hope that he could be of still greater service to him in that office.

The formal petition to found the Congregation had been addressed to Wiseman on St Charles' Day in the previous year, thus giving effect to his own wish. It was signed by the five priests and two clerics who formed the nucleus of the new congregation in order of seniority as follows:

> Henricus Eduardus Manning.
> Herbertus Vaughan *pro se et* Thoma McDonnell.
> Gulielmus Joannes Roberts.
> Gulielmus Burke.
> Carolus Joannes Laprimaudaye.
> *Pro* Henrico Arturo Rawes, H. E. Manning.

On Whit Sunday 1857, the infant community met for the first time at Bayswater in a rented house and the next day, having said their Masses in the unfinished church that Wiseman had made over to them, they held their first General Chapter. Of the three original founder-members Manning was, within a few months, the only survivor. Wilberforce had died in the February of that year and the third, Charles Laprimaudaye, Manning's former curate at Lavington, who had joined him in providing funds for purchasing the property which became the site of St. Edward's, Palace Street, died in Major Orders at Rome in the following January after nursing a fellow-student suffering from small-pox.

All seemed set fair for beginning the work undertaken in obedience to the Cardinal and with the blessing of the Holy See, and to that work the small band devoted all its zeal, energy and financial resources, with the result that within seven years Manning could summarize progress as follows: Whereas on coming to Bayswater in 1857 they had found an unfinished shell of a church served by one priest and a school-house without a school, there was now a community of twelve priests and nine students, one church completed and three built by

Oblates; eight schools accommodating 790 children, including a Reform School and a Choir School (out of which developed the future St Charles' College), four convents with fifty nuns, and in the establishment of these institutions upwards of £30,000 was contributed from the Fathers' private means and from the gifts of their personal friends; a record of achievement all the more remarkable when we remember that, far from being allowed to pursue its works in peace, the Congregation was, for the greater part of this time, caught up in a whirlwind of ecclesiastical strife which threatened its very existence.

The tempest had been brewing ever since the restoration of the Hierarchy and was ready to break at the moment the Oblates came into being. That they found themselves at the centre of the storm was chiefly due to the outstanding personality of Manning, whom Wiseman had chosen, and who was most willing to be, his champion in the bitter contests that had their origin in the difficulties which almost inevitably arose during the period of transition through which the Church in England had just passed.

The establishment of the Hierarchy did not fulfil all that had been hoped from it. The clergy gained little in status though they were to feel the greater weight of hierarchical pressure since the authority of the bishops had been strengthened. Wiseman himself, as Metropolitan, was inclined to keep too much control in his own hands and to exercise it autocratically. This brought him into conflict with the other bishops who were not slow to assert their rights. Moreover, his dedication of himself to the conversion of England and the form which his zeal in that direction took, especially the unbounded favour which he showed to the influx of converts, aroused the hostility of all ranks among the old Catholics, while his inattention to administrative matters, for which he had little taste or ability, resulted in general exasperation.

When Wiseman became aware of the turn things were taking, he tried to remedy matters by obtaining the appointment of Archbishop Errington, the ' old George ' of his student days and his right-hand man during his presidencies of the English College and Oscott, as his co-adjutor with right of succession. As to ability he could have made no better choice; as to compatibility he could have made no worse. For Errington was not only the antithesis of Wiseman in character and temperament, but as a Catholic of the old school he had no sympathy with his innovations and proselytizing zeal. This Wiseman knew well, but he trusted to their lifelong friendship to smooth over all difficulties. As usual he was too sanguine, and within six months the two Archbishops were at loggerheads over the conduct of diocesan affairs and a complete break was only avoided by Errington's departure to take temporary charge of the vacant See of Clifton.

It was during his absence that the formation of the Oblates was completed and by the time he was ready to return to his post in Westminster it was to find Manning installed as Provost of the Chapter and Herbert Vaughan, who had already been appointed as Vice-President of St Edmund's, now also an Oblate, as were three other members of the College staff, viz., Fr McDonnell and Fr O'Callaghan who became in turn Rector of the English College and Bishop of Hexham and Newcastle, and the saintly Robert Butler, later to be the Spiritual Prefect of St Edmund's where, at the request of his friend Bishop Ward, he now lies buried in the College Lady Chapel.

An Oblate high in the Diocesan Councils and others in charge of the training of the Church students of the Diocese— this was a state of affairs which the future Archbishop of Westminster [and that at no very distant date in view of Wiseman's failing health] was not prepared to accept. But it was necessary to act at once before the new Congregation received final approbation and confirmation; it was still on trial and might be found wanting, at least as to status. Well versed as he was in Canon Law, he was able to discover what both the collaborators, the Roman Canonists, the Prefect of Propaganda and even Pius IX in spite of his ' *senza voti*,' had apparently overlooked, viz., that the Oblates were a Religious Order, therefore their inclusion in the diocese was canonically irregular. But while as yet the ' hawk-like ' Errington might not swoop, Wiseman ' the old lion ' lay sleeping. Therefore ' in order to awaken him,' said Errington, ' it is necessary to bring every form of external pressure to bear upon him. One day he will awake, he will put out his paw and then he will drive them all away.' The pressure was exerted through the Westminster Chapter which, on the basis of Errington's findings, arraigned Manning as to the nature of the Oblates and their presence at St Edmund's and later drew up a petition to the Holy See for the removal of the Oblates from the College. This Manning was asked to sign as Provost of the Chapter. Upon his refusal, on the grounds that the matter was outside the competence of the Chapter, and despite Wiseman's nullification of the proceedings for the same reason, the petition was forwarded and thus began the Process which was to send Manning backwards and forwards to Rome for the next seven years, both in his own and in Wiseman's defence, and which ended in the deposition of Errington by Pius IX and in the appointment of Manning to the See of Westminster. Such was the ultimate and unlooked-for result of rousing ' the old lion.'

Of the years between, the ' years of famine,' as Manning called them—years of acute controversy with many wounds inflicted on both sides, of the clash of personalities, of the strategy and tactics of the protagonists—of all this the biographers of the period have treated extensively but with more stress on the dramatic highlights than on the underlying issues and with a tendency to anticipate not a little the Strachey method and ' to roam out over that great ocean of material and lower down into it, here and there, a little bucket, which will bring up to the light of day some characteristic specimen from those far depths to be examined with careful curiosity.' And as it is of such stuff that biographies are made, specimens they give us in plenty, but it is to Rome that we must for the final classification and labelling. There, the rampaging Irishman, the episcopal John Bull, the fighting parson, and the ecclesiastical Mrs. Malaprop would scarcely be recognizable even as caricatures. Nor would the hurly-burly tactics of this or that English playing-field avail for the winning of battles in the Roman Courts—nothing less would suffice than that superlative degree of diplomatic and forensic skill and dogged pertinacity displayed by Manning throughout the long years of legalistic dispute, by which he enhanced his reputation in Rome. So that in 1863 it could be said of him:

Mgr Manning has come out nobly this year in Rome. He has gained immensely in the opinion of the Pope and

I may say of the Cardinals. They are open-mouthed about him. He is looked upon by all as a first-rate man, especially since his discourse at the Trinità. He is certainly greatly improved and as different from what he was ten years ago as possible. He is much more *sciolto* and open. Everyone sees that he is called to do great things in England.

This report, coming as it does from the pen of the redoubtable Mgr Talbot, is not lacking in characteristic embellishment. But, though we may discount the rows of gaping Cardinals and be quite sure that Manning was no more *sciolto* than it suited him to be, yet it is reliable in so far as it shows that his success and prestige were gained in open forum and owed little to intrigue. Least of all was it due to slinking up the ' little winding stair ' and through the ' low arched door ' into that Victorian-Gothic corner of the Palazzo Vaticano designed for Mgr Talbot by architect Lytton Strachey and so admirably adapted for the hatching of plots and plans for the overthrow of the opponents of Wiseman and Manning. Whereas the worst that really happened was that the pen ran away with the Papal Secretary who, forgetting his true rôle of official and unofficial channel of information, took it upon himself to manage a Pope with ' a peculiar character,' a vacillating Roman Curia, a refractory English Hierarchy and its doubtful succession, with his services as mentor to all and sundry given gratis and without stint. All of which, entailing as it did the dropping of many bricks and the treading on one clerical toe after another, his correspondents did not find such fun as their many wry comments testify.

But the Pope, in spite of his many cares, could sometimes laugh, possessing as he did that characteristic which made him seem peculiar to the guileless Talbot, viz., a keen sense of humour which he often exercised at the expense of his ' *caro Giorgio* '—as witness his devastating remark when, contrary to all expectation, he appointed Manning to the See of Westminster: ' What a diplomatist you are to make what you wish come to pass! ' How little Talbot's wishful thinking influenced events is clear from his correspondence during the interim. For though he could mention many a name, even his own, as being among the likely candidates, Manning's was not included. Indeed in a letter to Canon

Morris he urges that any rumours as to the likelihood of Manning's succession should be completely discarded. Nevertheless it is characteristic that after the event he should divide the honour of the appointment between himself and the Holy Ghost. Michael Errington, the Archbishop's brother, who had every reason to measure the strength of the opposition, says of this same wily diplomat: ' If half be true of what is said of Roman duplicity, he is not fit for Rome.'

Whether the Kingdom of Heaven is also taken by diplomacy, especially of the kind exercised by Mgr Talbot, may be open to question. But it is quite certain that, as Manning had said several years previously: ' *Cognoscit suos Sedes Apostolica.*' It was hardly to be expected that the Holy See would regard the diffusion of the Roman spirit in English ecclesiastical circles as anything other than desirable, and Wiseman and Manning were the embodiment of that spirit. The Roman attitude regarding the old Catholics and the converts is best summed up in the words of Cardinal Marini: ' We know no such distinctions here.' Moreover it was Rome's mission to make converts, not to break them—least of all one of whom it could be said as Wiseman said of Manning: ' That in all England there is not another priest who in double the time has done what Dr Manning has for the advantage of the Catholic Church.' Nor is it surprising that in the last analysis the '*sempre docile*' Manning should be preferred to ' *quello benedetto Errington* ' who did not hesitate even to withstand Peter to the face—a line of action that has rarely succeeded in the Church especially when, as in this case, Peter was not shunning the Gentiles.

As to the spirit represented by Dr Errington and those who supported him, it was Manning's view that if it prevailed,

the work of the Church in England will be done by Religious, and the secular clergy will, for a generation to come, lose ground in all the points most essential for their action upon the people of England. They will continue to administer the Sacraments to the almost exclusively Irish population now in England, and the work and mission of the Church as contemplated by the Holy Father in the hierarchy, and as demanded by the state of England, and I will say by the manifest will of God, shown in his providential acts, will be thrown back for a whole generation.

It was this conviction that lay behind his resistance to the
conservatism of the old Catholic party and brought him so
wholeheartedly to the side of Wiseman whom he regarded as
the embodiment of the spirit of progress and missionary zeal.

To both of them the Hierarchy meant only one thing—
the body of bishops united under the leadership of Wiseman
as an instrument for the conversion of England. Both feared
that if this unity of purpose and action were lacking, then the
restoration of canonical rights and privileges might act as a
brake on missionary activity and result in the attitude: ' the
hierarchy is established, all's well with the Church in England.'
Thus the insistence of the bishops upon their rights and freedom
of action was dubbed ' Parliamentarianism ' by Wiseman who
regarded his primacy as being not only of honour but also
of jurisdiction, a view fully shared by Manning, who was
also of an authoritarian turn of mind. ' Otherwise,' he
wanted to know, ' what is the Pallium for? ' To him Wiseman was Rome in England and opposition to Wiseman he
regarded as opposition to the Holy See itself. ' We as Bishops
look at this from the light of our episcopal administration, you
from the side of the Holy See,' said Archbishop Ullathorne,
at that time a respected opponent as he was later to be a
valued friend—giving us at once the crux of the whole situation and the fundamental reason for Manning's overall
success before the Roman Tribunals, where the canonical
issues were judged on their merits, without favour to one party
or the other and with a deliberation that not all the fretting
and fuming of the contestants could influence or hasten. For
the Roman Canonists it was all in the day's work, for apart
from the personal feeling engendered and the conflicting
views on general policy, the points in dispute were largely the
outcome of the division of territory and jurisdiction—very
much in the nature of growing pains. Similar situations
occurred in America on the establishment of the Hierarchy,
while the question of the competence of Diocesan Chapters
was not confined to the Archdiocese of Westminster—Holland,
too, had its difficulties in this respect. There was even a
' St Edmund's incident ' on the Pope's own doorstep when the
Cardinal Bishop of Albano, wishing to place his diocesan
seminary provisionally in charge of a Religious, met with the

opposition of his Canons. Perhaps only the Edmundian Oblate to whom the story was told could fully appreciate the piquancy of that situation.

And none was more weary of the protracted negotiations than Manning who had to bear the brunt of them as Wiseman's agent. But not once did he falter or lose his canonical bearings and since he never wanted more than Rome was willing to give, he could accept even adverse decisions with equanimity. It was enough for him that they should be made by the one authority he regarded as supreme. He was vindicated on the point that touched him most deeply, viz., the Congregation of the Oblates of St Charles, whose continuation Pius IX had once said in ironic mood, ' depends on the Archbishop of Trebizond.' It would indeed have been ironical if Manning, who, throughout the whole of his Catholic life, was the champion of the secular clergy both as to their status and action, should have been guilty of the anomaly of foisting a Religious Order upon a diocese as an integral part of its life.

The removal of the Oblates from St Edmund's, advocated by Rome in order to restore good relations between Wiseman and the Westminster Chapter, and because of the opposition of Bishop Grant of Southwark who had a controlling interest in the College, while it was keenly felt by Manning, resulted directly in the foundation of St Joseph's Missionary College, Mill Hill, by Herbert Vaughan. Even as Vice-President of St Edmund's Vaughan had cherished the thought of introducing a certain number of Missionary students into the College, so that England might have some share in propagating the Faith in pagan lands, and as early as 1859 he opened his heart to Manning who, while wholly sympathetic, advised delay; and wisely so, as events turned out. But now the way was clear. Wiseman was enthusiastic, seeing in the project the fulfilment of one of the desires of his own youth. In November 1862 the resolution to form a Missionary College was passed by the Oblates in Chapter and in the next year Vaughan, having received the approbation of the English Hierarchy and the Holy See, was given leave of absence to collect funds in South America.

On hearing of Wiseman's death he wrote: ' Who is to continue the work of which he laid the foundations? . . . The only man I see is my Father Superior.' He was delighted, therefore, when he received news of Manning's appointment but was apprehensive as to the effect it might have on his own position. In June 1865 he was recalled to England by Manning and in a letter to his father he says: ' I am returning to England with some anxiety, scarcely knowing what to expect under the new régime . . . I shall be glad if I have not the responsibility of our House in Bayswater thrust upon me in part.' His fears were not without foundation for he was looked upon as Manning's natural successor by the Oblate Community and his name was first upon the *terna* at the election of the new Superior. But Manning chose the second nominee, Fr Dillon, who had acted as his Vicar during his long absences in Rome, and left Vaughan free to devote himself to the work upon which he had set his heart.

The biographies, taken up as they are with the controversial issues in which he was involved during the early period of his life and the wider horizons of later years, have little to say of Manning's relations with his fellow Oblates. But the Congregation and its well-being was his constant thought. During his many absences he kept in closest touch with every member, whether priest or student, in letters which show on his side how paternal an interest he took in them, consoling, encouraging or praising as the occasion demanded, and on theirs the filial and fraternal spirit which bound them together. F. C. Burnand assures us that it was no stern-faced ecclesiastic who joined in the Novices' recreation at Bayswater with a zest as boyish as their own. He also testifies to the fact that the venerable Doctor Manning was not altogether unappreciative of the early essays in humour displayed by the future Editor of *Punch*, while he scotches the apocryphal story that it was one of his efforts in this direction, viz., the shooting of paper pellets at the bald pate of the Fr Superior, which was the cause of his leaving the noviceship.

After he became Archbishop, Manning showed the same fatherly interest in the students at the House of Studies in Rome, and they tell of many kindnesses received from him and from Pius IX because of his friendship with Manning. There was, for example, the memorable occasion on which Manning received the Pallium, when the students were invited to break-

fast with the Pope, the Secretary of State, Cardinal Antonelli,
and the new Archbishop, when they partook of a very un-
Papal repast which included chocolate, coffee, buns, cakes and
ices; but in truly Papal style, being waited on by Monsignori,
several of whom afterwards became Cardinals, and a detachment of the Noble Guard with drawn swords in attendance
throughout the meal; a display of armed might which did not
prevent Mgr Talbot from sending the students away with
their pockets filled with bonbons which he had raided from
the Pope's table. Writing from Rome at this time Manning
speaks with pleasure of the happy family spirit which he found
among the students and of the good name they were making
for themselves in Roman circles.

For his successor, Fr. Dillon, and those who should follow
him, Manning drew up a rule of life for Superiors calculated
to satisfy the most exacting subject. It was as follows:

1. Try to be gentle, calm, silent as possible.
2. Never contradict anybody.
3. If you are forced to differ say: ' I should hardly
have thought so,' or ' I thought it was so and so,' or ' Can
you be sure that it is so?' Contradictions seldom convince
and almost always irritate.
4. Never reprove anyone in the presence of others.
5. Find all the excuses you can for them, that they
may be ashamed of excusing themselves.
6. Never refuse permission unless compelled and then
with gentleness, kindness and regret. Let them know that
you are going against yourself.
7. Try to cheer and amuse everybody especially if they
are ill, or in trouble or out of sorts, that they may turn to
you as the refugium and requies peccatorum.
8. Watch over your manner and tones of voice and look.
Be very courteous, considerate and delicate in dealing with
others, especially those you are a little impatient with.
9. Pray very much against prejudice and dislike of persons.
10. Look through the largest window in the house, not
through the keyhole.
11. In giving obedience don't order but ask. ' Be as
good as to do so and so.' ' Would you do so and so,' and
offer to do it sometimes yourself.

Here are ten commandments for you and one over.

In his address at the first Chapter following his appointment as Archbishop, Manning defined his future relations with the Community he had founded. *Semel oblatus* he would be *semper oblatus*, continuing to follow the Rule he had drawn up for them. The Congregation would be more closely united to him than ever before, since he was now their Superior in the fullest sense and dear as it had even been, dearer it would ever be. All men knew how he loved this place and the members of the Congregation, and they would be quick to notice any marks of predilection. Therefore any abstinence from outward marks of love and affection would have to be attributed to his sense of public duty; he must merge the private feelings which he held into consideration for the whole clergy of the diocese. But he would keep his room in Bayswater which he would always regard as home. And this he did until the end of his life. It was his custom to be present at the annual Chapter, giving an opening and closing address, while leaving the Fathers free to debate and vote upon the matters on the agenda, and while he was scrupulous in respecting the liberty of the Congregation as to its internal and domestic affairs, he was always as ready to give the benefit of his counsel and assistance as the Community was ready to receive it.

Sixteen years later he wrote in his journals:

> There remains one work in which I have hope and consolation above all others, I mean the Congregation of the Oblates of St Charles. It was begun almost blindly, so little did I see then what I see now. It was begun in obedience to my Bishop; it was shaped in Rome; it was specially blessed by Pius IX. It was at once sorely tried by a very formidable opposition. It was confirmed by the trial. If it had not been God's work it would never have endured the assault. The eight years I was at St. Mary's were the happiest of my life. Hard indeed and full of anxiety, but full of a high peace and independence of the world. My name has always been over my door and I never feel so much at home as when I am in that little room. I lived in it only eight years but those eight years were a work and a life which cannot be measured by dial time.

III

MANNING AND THE SEE OF
WESTMINSTER, 1865–1892

By Gordon Albion

D R Manning was in Rome when he received a telegram
sent at Wiseman's desire to return at all speed. He
arrived in time to tell the dying Cardinal that Pope
Pius IX had sent him his affectionate blessing. ' Thank him,
thank him, thank him.' No other word passed between the
first Archbishop of Westminster and his successor.

Whatever one might argue about Manning's ambition—
and even his many severe critics would concede his sincerity
in desiring high office, and the power it brings, only because
he was convinced of the good it would enable him to do—
Wiseman's Provost and confidant had no reason for thinking
he would succeed his master. He had been too closely, too
invidiously involved in the unhappy dispute between Wiseman
and his former coadjutor Errington, backed by the Westminster
Chapter. The ousting of Archbishop Errington to become a
mere parish priest in the Isle of Man and a professor at Prior
Park had taken on something of the aura of martyrdom, or
at any rate of victimization that could now be set right.

The Westminster Chapter sent to Rome a *terna* of names
headed by that of Errington while the two others, both bishops,
wrote in support of his candidature. This attempt by the
Chapter to secure a reversal of events was an obvious tactic
of self-vindication. Despite the general acclaim of the talents,
personality and achievements of the great Cardinal Wiseman,
there were many who had always opposed his large-hearted
sponsorship of the Oxford Converts, among whom he had been
convinced were the future leaders of the Church in England.
Their general opposition to this policy, pin-pointed in the
startlingly rapid promotion of the ex-Archdeacon of Chichester

to the Provostship of Westminster, became focused in a wide dislike and deep distrust of Manning. Although, for all these reasons, Manning was the last candidate the Westminster Canons would bring themselves to vote for, it should have been equally clear to them that the Holy See could hardly go back on its decisions of a few years before and elect Errington. However, there was another strong candidate in Ullathorne, the trusted friend and counsellor of his fellow-bishops, a sterling, pious and generally popular prelate, and highly thought-of in Rome through his long negotiations there for the Restoration of the Hierarchy. In fact, during the interim Manning himself wrote confidentially to Mgr George Talbot pressing for the appointment of Ullathorne or alternatively of Bishop Cornthwaite of Beverley.

But the Errington affair and the Chapter's opposition to Wiseman over the Oblates had given Manning's name prominence and prestige in Rome, where it was also known how strongly Wiseman had felt about having Manning to succeed him.

In the upshot history repeated itself. As in the cases of St Theodore, St Anselm and Stephen Langton, so now with Henry Edward Manning, the Pope set aside the recommendations from the home country and made the appointment a personal one of his own—and as in the other cases, a great pontificate justified the choice.

It was certainly a bold decision on the part of Pius IX to appoint to the newly created See of Westminster and to the leadership of a Hierarchy still winning its spurs, a man who had been married, was a convert and not a bishop.

But if these and his unpopularity with the clergy were disadvantages, overriding all in the eyes of the Holy See were Manning's enthusiasm for all that was Roman, his Oxford background, his qualities as a diplomat and, most of all, as a born ruler of men. Other and finer qualities were to dissipate the initial prejudice against Manning in England as they won general recognition: his profound faith, his genuine piety, his integrity, courage and singleness of purpose and, unexpectedly, his approachability.

The first intimation of the appointment came when the new Archbishop's priest-nephew, William Manning, found him

in tears kneeling before the Blessed Sacrament. His spiritual
reading during his pre-consecration retreat was Challoner's
Memoirs of Missionary Priests. Both these incidents are
revealing of Manning's anticipation of the trials that lay
ahead of him.

Ullathorne's reaction was characteristically in lighter vein;
he wrote saying that one reason for his own satisfaction at the
appointment was that there would now be one Monsignor less
in England. It was Ullathorne who was chosen for the
consecration that took place at St Mary Moorfields on June 8,
1865—the place and date Wiseman had planned to celebrate
his own episcopal silver jubilee. Bishop Amherst of Northampton preached the sermon. It was on the Holy Ghost—a
subject of Manning's dearest devotion. The strain of the occasion, added to ill-health and a natural pallor, provoked an
audible comment from the crowd: ' Why have they given us
an Archbishop with one foot in the grave? ' Manning's reply
came quickly: ' I think I have a dozen more years of work in
me yet! ' Apparently he really thought that, but his forecast
was an underestimate by more than half. In accordance with
custom, as he had not yet received the Pallium, Manning
continued to style himself Archbishop-Elect until told by
Propaganda to drop the adjective. Later in the year he went
to Rome to petition for the Pallium and it was there
that Pius IX told Manning that many people had advised
him for a variety of reasons not to make the appointment
but that a ' voice ' kept whispering to him: ' Put him
there, put him there.' Manning himself told the story in
confidence to his secretary, Fr John Morris, later of the
Society of Jesus.

It was natural that the new Archbishop, who had in a sense
been prepared for his task by Wiseman and had preached
at his funeral a sermon in which he graphically assessed the
achievements of the past pontificate, should inaugurate a
memorial to his great predecessor, deciding that it should
take the form of a Cathedral to be as large as Notre Dame
in Paris.

It was characteristic of Manning that having secured a
splendid site for the Cathedral, he determined to leave the
actual building to his successor and to devote all his energies

to a task outwardly less attractive but far dearer to the heart of the true pastor that he was. Manning's pontificate of twenty-seven years has been described with some truth as ' The Battle for Catholic Education.' It became his main preoccupation and with the slogan ' Schools before Churches ' he decided he would not spend a penny on the projected Cathedral for Westminster till every Catholic child in his diocese was placed in a Catholic school. He at once founded the Westminster Diocesan Education Fund and some fourteen years later was able to say: ' The work for poor children may be said to be done. . . . There is school room for all.'

A drastic campaign became necessary with the passing of Forster's Elementary Education Act of 1870. This established School Boards all over the country and for the first time elementary education became compulsory: with the result that new schools had to be provided everywhere for the vast number of children who up to that time had never attended school.

The alternative before Catholics was to provide their proportion of new schools or see their children forced to attend the non-denominational Board Schools. Under Manning's energetic leadership the whole English Catholic body, bishops, clergy and wealthy laity, rose to the occasion. In a nation-wide campaign, public meetings were held and large sums of money subscribed. The crisis fund under Lord Howard of Glossop eventually provided for 70,000 children at a cost of £350,000. An era of Catholic school-building had begun and the grave threat to the ideal of Catholic education proved in the end a powerful means of consolidating and strengthening the faithful. At his accession Manning estimated that he would have to provide orphanages for 20,000 Catholic children without relatives or friends.

Twenty-five years later, in his Lenten Pastoral of 1890 the aged Archbishop announced that the poor children of his diocese were provided for as follows: 23,000 were on the books of the parochial schools and 4,542 had been entirely provided for in homes, while, between 1868 and 1889, 10,000 workhouse Catholic children had been transferred to Catholic schools as a result of a prolonged struggle with the Metropolitan Board of Guardians. When the Free Education Act of 1891 was passed, Manning saw the partial success of what he had been urging by voice and pen for so many years.[1]

In 1873, after a lapse of fourteen years, the provincial meetings started by Wiseman were resumed when Manning held the Fourth Council of Westminster at St Edmund's College, Ware, from July 21 to August 12. The decrees reveal again the preoccupation with elementary, secondary and university education. The Catholic University College and several diocesan seminaries projected were realized with varying degrees of success in subsequent years.

Manning himself, who had been made a Cardinal in 1875, set the example with the short-lived Hammersmith Seminary (now the Sacred Heart Convent) opened in 1884 under Dr Weathers.

Ullathorne opened a Seminary at Olton that was later sold to the Capuchins, but Bishop O'Reilly built a Seminary at Upholland that still serves the diocese of Liverpool, and in 1889 Bishop Butt of Southwark began at Henfield and soon transferred to Wonersh a model Tridentine seminary, whose first rector, Fr Francis Bourne, made there a name for himself that took him rapidly through the See of Southwark to Westminster and the Cardinalate.

Similar attempts in the dioceses of Salford, Nottingham and Leeds failed to last. A more successful venture, first blessed by Wiseman and encouraged to the full by Manning, was the zealous enterprise of one of the latter's Oblates and closest friend, Fr Herbert Vaughan, in founding, with funds collected on a world tour, the Foreign Missionary College at Mill Hill, London. It was opened in March 1871 with a community of thirty-four and has grown from strength to strength, fed by schools at Rosendaal in Holland and Freshfield near Liverpool.

In the sphere of higher education for the laity Manning's policy was unfortunate. With influential backing, Newman planned to found a Catholic Hall at Oxford whither his

---

[1] Statistics show with what determination Manning kept to his slogan of 'Schools before Churches.' During his pontificate (1865-1892) the number of churches and Mass centres in the archdiocese increased from 117 to 129, an increase of 10 per cent.; clergy from 214 to 354, an increase of just over 60 per cent.; while the number of poor children attending Catholic elementary schools jumped 100 per cent. These are the figures:—1865: Present at inspection, 11,145; Average attendance, 11,112. 1891-2: Present at inspection, 22,552; Average attendance, 21,776.

prestige would attract Catholics, but this promising scheme was adamantly opposed by Manning on the grounds that Oxford was at that time drifting into a whirlpool of free thought and rationalism—dangerous waters for impressionable Catholic youth to embark upon. As Manning's views were bitterly contested, he appealed to the Holy See for a ruling, with the result that Newman's project was disallowed and Catholic parents might send their sons to the English universities only by special leave obtained from their Ordinary.

In circumstances of less tension Manning's policy was reversed by his successor with leave from Rome and with what have proved the happiest results. Meanwhile, Manning made a determined attempt to provide a University training for and by Catholics by starting a college at Kensington where students could read for external degrees from the University of London.

The Rector chosen was Mgr Capel, a popular preacher but otherwise little qualified for his task. Yet he was given a supporting staff of outstanding Catholic scholars; F. A. Paley, a Cambridge convert, lectured in Classics; Barff in Chemistry; St George Mivart in Biology; C. S. Devas in political economy; Dr Robert Clarke in modern philosophy; Gordon Thompson in English literature; Croke Robinson in Church history.

The project was pushed with Manning's usual energy and tenacity, which obtained for it substantial financial backing from a nation-wide collection and the generosity of wealthy Catholics, but it was never popular and the number of students never exceeded forty-five. It must be confessed that the main cause of the failure was Manning's obstinately short-sighted and small-minded refusal to employ the two most powerful, indeed the only forces that could have ensured the success of such a scheme—Newman and the Jesuits. So after a few years the college was closed and the balance of funds turned over to other educational purposes.

Another of Manning's enterprises in Catholic education was St Charles's College, Bayswater, run by the Oblates, his own foundation. After a period of popular success under Mgr William Manning, the Cardinal's nephew, and then under Dr Butler, his friend and confessor, the school buildings were made over to the Sacred Heart Nuns who used them as a training college for teachers.

The greatest event of Manning's pontificate was the Vatican Council of 1870 and the distinguished rôle played by Manning in its historic meetings was as a bishop and therefore belongs strictly to an account of his episcopate.

He was one of the 500 bishops present in Rome for the eighteenth centenary of SS Peter and Paul and heard Pius IX proclaim his intention of convening a General Council.

He was back in Rome for its opening on December 8, 1869, and was made a member of the Committee ' De Fide,' to which was referred in March 1870 the question of Papal Infallibility. All the force of Manning's personality was brought to bear in influencing the passing of the decree of July 18. Although he only spoke twice at the Council his influence was potent behind the scenes. Through Lord Odo Russell, then British Minister at the Court of Rome, he was able to counteract the efforts of Döllinger and Lord Acton to win over Gladstone to a policy of diplomatic interference.

In Rome he worked energetically to organize the voting for the Definition. He faced a harder task in England where the ' Inopportunists ' had the sympathy of Newman and a group of distinguished converts as well as the strong support of Lord Acton.

Among English Protestants the opposition was extreme, led by Prime Minister Gladstone whose pamphlet *The Vatican Decrees* maintained that civil allegiance was incompatible with belief in Papal Infallibility. It was Manning's duty to answer this caricature by a lucid exposition of the doctrine, which he did in three pastoral letters entitled *Petri Privilegium* and later in his *True Story of the Vatican Council* (1878). These writings and Newman's *Letter to the Duke of Norfolk* (1875), also a reply to Gladstone's strictures, did much to remove Protestant misconceptions and to scotch the hoary libel that a loyal Catholic cannot be a loyal Englishman.

The vigour of Cardinal Manning's work at the Vatican Council and his championship of its decrees won him such prestige that in the 1878 Conclave that elected Leo XIII, he was given a vote or two himself—the first time an English name had been mentioned in connection with the Papacy since the days of Cardinal Pole. The story of English newspaper correspondents that Manning had been canvassing his own candidature was considered sufficiently ridiculous by his fellow-Cardinals for them to twit him about it.

In the new Pope Manning found a social reformer of like mind to his own and he was soon to find many of his most cherished convictions stated with papal authority in the great *Rerum Novarum* which beyond all doubt owes something to his counsel and advice.

The Archbishop had soon to seek for himself the help of Pope Leo in a matter that was causing him considerable anxiety in the government of the Church in England. At the 1877 Low Week meeting of the Hierarchy, he proposed the presentation of a petition to the Holy See to determine the relationship between the bishops and the regular clergy, particularly in the thorny problem of episcopal visitation of missions run by regulars and control of mission funds. The result of Manning's initiative was the Constitution *Romanos Pontifices* of 1881, whose provisions were extended later to most English-speaking countries.

As old age forced the Cardinal to withdraw from the heat of controversy that consumed so much of his earlier energy, his influence increased rather than diminished, for even his critics cannot gainsay his Christlike compassion for the poor and the outcast. He was invited to sit on the Royal Commission on the Housing of the Working Classes, 1884–1885, and by the express desire of the Prince of Wales was placed next in precedence to His Royal Highness.

He had long won the respect of the Irish by his strong support of Home Rule, and the passionate zeal with which he promoted the ' League of the Cross,' a total abstinence organization, did immense good in combating the drink evil then playing terrible havoc among the Irish poor of East London. The ravages of intemperance were brought home to him by his reading of the Reports of a Committee of the House of Commons and, once convinced that the ' Pledge ' was a remedy, he took it himself in 1873 and delivered a series of temperance speeches, which were later published. His campaign produced a number of stories which the Cardinal loved to tell against himself. A remark that he never drank save under doctor's orders was met by the sally ' Change your doctor.' On another occasion he asked a man if he had taken the Pledge and was told: ' No, my confessor says I do not need it.' ' But I have taken it,' said the Cardinal. ' Perhaps you needed it,' came the reply.

The incident whereby Manning's name will always be best remembered among Englishmen was the ' Cardinal's Pence,' his successful mediation with the Port of London Dockers whose strike in 1889 had apparently reached deadlock till Manning's patient persuasiveness induced the men to accept terms.

Among his clergy their Archbishop had never been a popular figure but their earlier mistrust changed to a deep reverence for the self-denying ascetic whose ' palace ' was a ' famous place for catching colds ' and who himself practised the high ideals he set before them in his spiritual classic *The Eternal Priesthood*. His eager sponsorship of the title ' Father ' instead of the hitherto customary ' Mister ' for the diocesan clergy sufficiently indicates what he wanted them to be in relation to their people.

' The Cardinal was himself above all a ' *Pater Pauperum* '— ' An Archbishop who lived among his people. The doors of his house were worn with the footsteps of the fatherless and the widowed, the poor, the forlorn, the tempted and the disgraced, who came to him in their hours of trouble and sorrow.'

Their final tribute was paid in the popular demonstration along the whole line of his funeral route—a striking testimony to the warm place won in the hearts of all by this one-time controversial and, to some, repellent prelate, who was at last seen by all to be a holy man, single-minded in the service of his Master.

IV

MANNING AND HIS FRIENDS

By SHANE LESLIE

FROM Harrow and Oxford onwards Manning knew how to make friends from amongst the best. If the sons of great merchants were sent to Eton and Harrow to make influential friends, Manning profited by the venture. At Oxford he was described as the most popular man after Sidney Herbert, and there he enjoyed a life as select and sheltered as the unreformed House of Commons.

At Harrow his friends were the Bevans and Oxendens and Wordsworths and from Ireland the future Bishop Leslie of Kilmore, whose family long kept Manning's schoolboy letters. Leslie's great grandfather had written the book against Deism which Manning learnt at Harrow, and wrote: ' I took in the whole argument and I thank God that nothing has ever shaken it.'

Manning's best friend in school days was John Anderdon, his brother-in-law, who financed and advised him on the road to Oxford. Their correspondence taught Manning to subject the flowery and the whimsical to style. Anderdon was his philosopher and friend.

At Balliol Manning found important friendship flowering at every step. In the rooms of Charles Wordsworth, future Bishop of Lincoln, he met Gladstone and knitted a friendship which was intimate and enduring until Manning seceded from Anglicanism. Together they competed for the Newdigate Prize, writing grammatical but unsuccessful verse about *Coeur de Lion*. Together they studied the Anglican Fathers like the ' Judicious ' Hooker. Together they came under the Oxford Movement, for Newman was then Vicar of St. Mary's. Through the friendship of their fathers Manning became close with Samuel Wilberforce, his future brother-in-law. His friends were all future Churchmen but then the cream of the Universities had begun reading for Holy Orders. It was a rich field for the Church. It is difficult to imagine how many men of first-class ability were aiming at Rectories, Canonries, Deaneries as the best outlet for life and talent at that time.

Milnes Gaskell in a book called *Records of an Eton Schoolboy* gives an account of his father at Oxford writing of ' the man who, with the exception of Sidney Herbert, is more deservedly popular than anyone I know—Manning of Balliol. Manning is very unassuming and perhaps the best-informed man in Oxford.'

Manning saw Life steadily and saw it whole. He saw all earthly friendships *sub specie eternitatis*, human on one side but in their divine relationship on the other. He wrote that beautiful simile:

As in a piece of tapestry, where on one side all is a con-fused and tangled mass of knots, and on the other a beautiful picture, so from the everlasting hills will this earthly life appear not the vain and chanceful thing men deem it here, but a perfect plan guided by a Divine Hand unto a perfect end.

Of all his Oxford friends Gladstone was undoubtedly the closest and, while Manning remained Anglican, they corre-sponded intimately and the Archdeacon became godfather to the Statesman's son William Henry. How Gladstone had yearned to make him Archbishop of Canterbury appears in his everlasting regrets over Manning's conversion. In later time the Bishop of Winchester (Talbot) remained with Gladstone at Hawarden after the sudden death of Archbishop Benson in 1896 in the local church and recorded that Gladstone spoke incessantly about Manning, whose life by Purcell had just appeared. Gladstone's view was that in the Catholic Church Manning for the first time had a free hand to employ his special gifts for management. In the Church of England he would have found Parliament and the Privy Council against him. Hence his change.

Manning's closest friend while he was an Anglican curate and Archdeacon was Gladstone. Their immense corre-spondence was all in all to each. The crash came in 1851. There used to be a little chapel off Buckingham Palace Road (now replaced by a cinema!) where the two friends knelt for the last time together. Manning rose saying he could no longer take the Communion in the Church of England. Gladstone remained. One of the great Victorian friendships had been severed.   Henceforth Gladstone regarded him as one who had murdered his mother.   Manning found no approach to his old friend except in the political field when they held the uneasy relations of a Cardinal to a Prime Minister of England.

It must be remembered of Manning's friendships that none were frivolous, not even his cricketing alliances with other Harrovians.   He required his friends to tread with him to a higher level.   His converse was exalted and he turned instinctively to the higher things of Church and State.   It was a time when winds heralding immense progress and spiritual movements blew across the thought of an awakening country.

The Cardinal had been married during the short years when the delicate Miss Sargent had lived.   This had softened his deep asceticism and his feelings for women both in Anglican and Catholic days.   He advised them living and guarded their secrets dead.   Perhaps the most remarkable had been Florence Nightingale whom he had advised and helped when she set out on her mission to the Crimea.   Most of her letters to Manning have been published though few of his have survived.   One is significant towards the close of their friendship (April 22, 1861):

> I have letters of yours among my papers and I will put them together.   But be sure that the knowledge of your wish will prevent my giving them into any hand and at my death every letter, paper and journal of mine will be burnt unopened.   This charge will be religiously executed by the Fathers of our Congregation.   I have no need to fear officious inkbottles but so much private matter may be found in my papers that not a scrap will escape the fire. Many thanks, all my affairs have prospered beyond my hope.   Four years have given us 3 Churches, 4 Convents and Schools and a Community in Fathers and Novices of four and twenty.   But we have steamed out to sea against a storm and since I saw you I have gone through more than I ever thought could come upon me.   The end has been complete.   Your question must excuse my saying so much.

Florence Nightingale was fascinated like many other distinguished women by Manning.   He gave them an exquisite friendship that the mother of Augustus Hare described as ' the harmony of religious poetry.'

None could predict where the Oxford Movement would lead. Friends stood hand in hand awaiting the dawn. Though Manning had turned from politics and commerce, which were both open to him, into the loneliness of a Sussex curacy, he was possessed of a splendid array of friends in both Low and High Church. Amongst the Evangelicals were the Wilberforces and Bevans. The Bevans had brought him to religious conversion in their manner.

During Anglican days he was devoted to Sidney Herbert, the Sir Galahad of the Victorians. In the Church he was devoted to Archdeacon Hare but many more were accounted his nameless friends among the humble shepherds and toilers under the Downs.

When the trial of conversion approached, many high and mighty friends fell away. In those days to range yourself with Rome made socially as great a cleft as conversion to Communism to-day. It meant a parting of friends and a scission of family ties. Manning's family were strongly divided and his friends even more so. He really brought over as friends none except those who accompanied him to Rome like Henry Wilberforce, William Anderdon and his curate Laprimaudaye. At the actual reception into new pastures the splendid presence of James Hope stood beside him.

Hope remained his friend but gradually gave his closer intimacy to Newman. Hope's funeral service in Farm Street presented the rare scene of Manning and Newman meeting as cardinals. Manning presided and Newman uttered a few words of farewell.

With Gladstone there was never intimacy again; only correspondence on subjects of vital interest to each other. Gladstone was always anxious to bring Ireland into tune with Great Britain and courted Hierarchies almost instinctively. Manning naturally was eager to turn the old friendship with Gladstone to Church service at home and abroad. Hence the flow of somewhat starchy letters to the end. One letter Gladstone ended: ' I venture to observe that I do not find your printed paper clear on the relations between *testimony* and *authority*: a remark which I hazard with hesitation because in general I think that one of the strongest points of your writings is their admirable clearness.'

One Anglican friend who has escaped Manning's biographers—at least the letters written to him by the Archdeacon have not been published—was an Eton Master, Edward Coleridge. They are worth quoting.

(Oct. 28, 1845) Our dear friend Newman has, at last, taken the step we have so long feared. Long as we have looked for it, I can hardly realize it as an event done and over. It is a heavy sorrow, which will stand alone, having nothing like it. How can we be surprised if it should affect many minds? And yet it seems to me that it ought not. Natural as it is, that one to whom we owe so much should powerfully affect us by every step he takes.

(Nov. 14, 1848) I am not disposed to censure the Church of England, but I cannot deny admiration to the Church of Rome. When shall we deal lovingly and truly with each other? On both sides we seem Masters in maligning.

(Nov. 1, 1850) The only point is, are we in obedience to the will of Jesus Christ in the Unity and Faith of His Church? If so, all contradictions on earth are nothing. And yet no-one will look this in the face. But I will not go on into it. I only wish you to know that nothing less than this could weigh with me in such a trial of faith and patience.

It is unfortunate that we know so little about this friendship between Harrovian and Etonian. Coleridge was the closest channel between old Eton and the Catholic revival.

In later years the Cardinal softened in his Anglican relations. Friends in the Church of England found themselves constantly correspondents or visitors. Deans and bishops wrote to him as though they were still proud of one who had been numbered in their company. A curious friendship arose with a distinguished Yorkshire layman, Sir Tatton Sykes, who spent a large fortune in spreading Gothic churches in the Ridings. His wife, Lady Sykes, had become a Catholic and for that reason he had toyed with the possibility of building the new Cathedral at Westminster, provided of course it was built in Gothic design. The Cardinal was much gratified by the prospect of filling the large empty site which had been purchased by the alms of the faithful. The plan eventually fell through when Sir Tatton insisted on reproducing the *Votif Kirche* in Vienna, which was found to be impossible.

It is not surprising that the old Committee became mystified and we find letters exchanged between the Duke of Norfolk and the Cardinal which do not appear to be known. The Duke, a very close and admiring friend, wrote (Jan. 18, 1885): ' I was startled the other day by someone remarking that it was proposed to dispose of a portion of the site and that, if this were done, the orientation would be impossible. I quite feel that your Eminence must to a certain extent be in Sir Tatton's hands in this matter as he is going to build the Church but I should think you might suggest to him that the subscribers to the original site ought to have their views consulted and that he would probably quite feel this.' The Cardinal answered next day: ' I am sorry you should be misled by rumours or letters as to the land for the Cathedral: and I should be still more sorry if you should think me to be in any way in Sir Tatton Sykes' hands. We have exhausted every plan and design to find the possibility of getting the necessary length E and W. It is not possible: and if possible would require an immense increase in price. We must therefore be content with the example of St. Peter's, St. Maria Maggiore and half the chief Churches of Rome.'

Among non-Catholic friends Sir Charles Dilke must be accounted high. No doubt the possible successor to Gladstone appealed to Manning as a useful acquaintance in the future. The Cardinal was anxious to keep in touch with the Radicals over the School Question. Dilke was anxious that the Cardinal should be interested in Labour questions, then very much below the surface of what Liberals thought sufficient for working men. The Cardinal was never a Liberal but he came near to a Christian Socialism.

Very sympathetic, though allied with a slight sternness, was the Cardinal's friendship with the pioneers of the English Labour movement such as John Burns and Ben Tillett. In his later days he was more sympathetic to the English workers and their struggling leaders than he was with old English Catholics like Herbert Vaughan and the Duke of Norfolk. The clearest account of his dealings with the Labour men and the London Dock Strike of 1889 was given in Mr. Bodley's Essay on the Cardinal. Bodley like Mr. Wilfrid Meynell had acted as confidential adviser to the Cardinal and to both these Men of Letters he could outpour his feelings on social questions as he never could to the English Hierarchy.

When Bodley's book was published Lady Dilke wrote to him:

I have been carefully reading your Manning and I am very glad that you have found time to put before us so just an image of the Cardinal's being and doing in what I think was perhaps the most complete episode in his life—it is the one passage in which we find his immense gift of human sympathy fulfilling itself uncontradicted by the conditions of the work he had in hand.

' Misery and suffering,' you say, ' caused him always the acutest anguish.' This was true in a degree that I have known in hardly any other man. I have heard him speak with a sound in his voice and a light in his eyes which meant depths of restrained passion. ' Give all yourself to London, it is the abomination of desolations ' or ' No one knows the depth of the sufferings of women save the doctor or the priest.' That he was so pained by your pain was the chief cause of his great power. He never could have been a great doctor of the Church, a great theologian for his metaphysics were of the weakest, but his brilliant understanding and unrivalled practical instincts coupled with this passionate capacity for feeling made him one of the striking personalities I have known.

His *first* movement was always right and noble, but it was *unreasoning* and he had a painful distrust of ' unreasoned ' impulse for his reason was very keen and appreciated at their highest value all the maxims of worldly experience. Sometimes it was as if he—in fear of being arrested by his own emotions—took refuge in the calculations of a pure worldly wisdom in its first expression almost cynical but always finally clothed in the language of a high morality. If his impulse took him counter to strong social prejudices he instinctively shrank before them. ' They don't care.'

It is quite true—as you quote from Mr Holland— that at the time when the strike broke out he knew little as to the rights or wrongs of the struggle. Nay more, as far as I know, he never came to a clear idea of the broader issues of Trade Unionism, though he put his name on our Committee in 1887 in order to strengthen my hands in dealing with ' his girls ' and though we had much talk about organization and kindred matters both as regarded London and the country.

V

MANNING AND NEWMAN

By Shane Leslie

THE divergence of Manning from Newman throughout their lives will always fill a paragraph in any history of the Catholic revival. They were the two protagonists from the beginning. Their Oxford friendship was a distant one between scholars, High Churchmen and College Dons with apostolic leanings. Little could they have foreseen how often their lives were fated to clash and how seldom to unite. Each in turn was hailed as the champion of the Church of England, if she was to stand in days of Reform Bills and changing beliefs. This only they really had in common that each in turn submitted to Rome and upon each in turn successive Popes conferred the Red Hat. Their relations remained those of highly strung, eager ecclesiastical leaders, varying immensely in talents and outlook and in their immediate purposes.

On almost every subject possible Newman and Manning remained temperamentally averse to one another. This had showed itself as early as in Oxford days when Manning claimed that he was outside the Oxford Movement led by Newman. Certainly he did not follow him out of the Church of England in 1845 but waited till 1851, when he characteristically said he had become a Catholic off his own bat! This was a phrase reminiscent of the faraway days when he was a cricketer and captain of the Harrow Eleven. It would be difficult to imagine Newman in the field. Manning is generally supposed to have remained outside the Tractarians, but it is worth recording that he shared anonymously in writing one of the Tracts with Charles Marriott. In his staid Anglican days he considered Newman's famous *Tract Ninety* as too clever or rather not straightforward. He retired into a Sussex curacy leaving Newman to carry on with his Movement. Thence he criticized Newman's *Sermons* in which he found 'something very

unsatisfactory . . . and cramping the cheering spirit of our
better hope.'

It is curious in how many ways their minds and moods
diverged. This was apparent in numberless ways, but never
more so than when they emerged to take part in public life.
In their early days of conversion each was busy selecting a
Religious Order in which to gather friends and followers.
The Oratory of St Philip Neri suited Newman to perfection,
and Manning always said that the eight years in which he
guided a House of the Oblates of St Charles were the happiest
of his life.

The Crimean War gave them the first opportunity to show
their talents and how very different they were! Newman's
attitude to the war was historical and intellectual. He lectured
on the *Turk in Europe* for whose benefit the war was largely
waged. Manning realized that the Church was offered a
golden opportunity to enter heroically into the national life.
He threw himself ardently into the work of despatching
Catholic chaplains to the Army and providing nursing Sisters
for the wounded.

Studying the two temperaments, it appears as though in the
interests not only of Catholic but of controversial unity that
Manning tried very hard to understand Newman but made a
wrong diagnosis. Newman on the other hand appreciated
Manning's character so little that he would not make a diagnosis
at all.

Manning's elevation to the Archbishopric made Newman
reconsider his feelings. Unfortunately there were a number
of matters on which Catholic leaders had to take side in the
Sixties such as the University Question and the Infallibility.
The question whether English Catholics could attend Oxford
or Cambridge was pivoted on the personal one whether
Newman should return to Oxford. In two quarters this was
regarded with dread: Dr. Pusey's Anglican sanctum and
Archbishop's House in Westminster. Already Newman had
sighed over the misunderstandings which befell him in the
Catholic camp. ' Faber, being taken away, Ward and
Manning take his place. Through them, especially Manning,
acting on the poor Cardinal, the Oxford Scheme has been
thwarted.'

In his dogmatic way Manning had made the exclusion of Catholics from the Universities a principle which he imposed not only at home but on Rome, where Oxford was never understood except in terms of a continental University.

Newman hoped to establish an Oratory at Oxford, which Manning could not forbid. The question was whether Newman's presence would attract Catholics. Newman wrote to Ullathorne (April 22, 1867): ' The answer will be as fallacious as the question is ensnaring unless I add my going will in fact attract Catholics there.' It was clear that Ulla-thorne was backing Newman but Manning insisted that it could not be isolated to the diocese for it affected the whole Church in England.

Here Manning's view was short-sighted compared with Newman's. Only a handful of Catholics dared attend the Universities, though a Cricket Blue was the bait which drew one. None lost their faith but Manning wrote about their losing humility and modesty, which was far from the case. Subconsciously Manning did not welcome the idea of Newman returning to enjoy an Oxford triumph. To carry out his attack on the Oxford scheme, logically Manning had to offer querulous Catholics some form of higher education. He spent thousands erecting such a House in Cromwell Road (not attractive to Irish), the boulevard of Kensington. He would have done better to have called in the Jesuits who have shown that they could support a University College by themselves in Dublin. Manning believed that young Catholics sought social functions and ' latchkeys in Grosvenor Square.' He therefore placed Mgr Capel, an exuberant favourite of Society, at the head. The fashionable side proved fatal and Capel had to be suspended. The failure was complete. Though Bishops and laity said plenty, Newman was silent.

Both believed the other had stood in the path and caused frustration of varied kind. Newman mourned in secret that he was withheld from Oxford. Manning also felt a personal disparagement. He wrote:

> My name was never mentioned, but his was brought in to condemn me; his name was never mentioned but mine was brought in to despite me. If only we had stood side by side and spoken the same thing, the dissension, division and

ill-will which we have had would never have been; and
the unity of Catholic truth would have been irresistible.
But it was not to be so.

Manning would not admit that Newman could ever differ
from him in the Faith: ' We diverged on public duties. My
line was not my own. It is that of the Bishops in 1862, 1867,
of the Holy See and of the Vatican Council.' Manning had a
wonderful way of comprehension: but the bishops of England
were far from believing he always represented their views.
The views of the Holy See, on which he laid such stress, were
more or less the opinions he had pressed upon Rome.

Ullathorne continued the wise duty of holding the scales
between Manning and Newman. It is history that finally he
let them sink in Newman's favour. He was Newman's bishop
and protector but Manning was his Metropolitan. The
balance became agitated when Newman became involved in
a public duel with Pusey. It was their opinions which
affected Englishmen's minds for or against Rome. Pusey
naturally made play with the Ultramontanism of Faber and
Manning. It was for Newman to explain that Ultramontanism was not the sole ladder to the Church. Ullathorne
was busy visiting the Oratorians or soothing Manning. He
wrote (February 14, 1866): ' I know that they are much
pleased with a little note you have sent; and I know that since
your elevation they have been thoroughly loyal to you.'
This letter was crossed in the post by Manning writing on the
same date: ' I wrote to thank him for the patristic part about
Our Lady, which is very well done and will do much good
among Anglicans, I hope. Dr. Newman's answer to my
note was the driest possible, and left any impression
that you say.'

Ward had prepared a severe criticism of Newman in the
Dublin Review which Manning suppressed, writing to Ullathorne (March 24, 1866): ' It is not published because of my
desire, with which Mr. Ward complied most promptly and
with a true Catholic yielding of his own will and judgement.
You will easily understand my reasons.'

Ullathorne pointed out that a layman had no business
criticizing a priest at all. ' I told Dr. Newman what you had

done and read to him that part of your letter which I felt would be satisfactory to him' and later (May 9, 1866) he rubbed a barb into Manning's lay henchman: 'I should care less if people did not persist in making you the sponsor of Mr. Ward. People say that if he had been a confessor, he would not be in a hurry to make mortal sins out of theological inferences.'

Manning took rebuke from Ullathorne and suppressed a book of his own for fear of collision with Newman which so surprised Newman that he wrote: 'Is it possible that Manning himself has changed? He is so close that no one can know.'

Manning seemed to Newman to be running with the Oratorian hare ('wrote me flattering letters') while hunting with the Ultramontane hounds ('privately sending for approval an article in which I was severely handled'). Manning was always striving to reconcile his duty as Archbishop with his friendship for Newman. In the end Newman accepted the duty ('I put aside the Archbishop, of course, because of his office') but put an end to the friendship in one quick phrase. He complained that in his dealings with Manning he never knew whether he was standing on his head or his feet! As Manning noted: 'terms which made a reply hardly fitting on my part. For years we never wrote and never met.'

They do not appear to have met at the Vatican Council which both attended, and the years passed. They were outwardly reconciled when Gladstone made his stirring attack on Vaticanism. It was the grief of a great Anglican who realized that the Vatican Council had destroyed his hopes for the unity of Christendom. It was Newman who answered Gladstone in his famous Letter to the Duke of Norfolk. Manning realized that Newman was the chosen champion and induced Ward to praise him in the *Dublin*: but Roman critics, never at home with Newman's subtle English, laid complaints against passages. Manning sent Cardinal Franchi a tremendous defence of Newman's orthodoxy as well as some prudential reasons for leaving Newman alone. Manning's letter to Cardinal Franchi remained secret but had a signal influence on Roman opinion. It was the beginning of a change at headquarters in Newman's favour (February 9, 1875).

However anxious Manning was to see Newman respected and valued in Rome and however much he took upon himself to further his comfort and position at home, fate chose him to obstruct the two achievements most dear to Newman. He really had longed to return to Oxford and when the Cardinal's Hat was offered him by Leo XIII he did not wish to refuse it though undoubtedly Manning put that construction on a certain letter, which furthermore he must have sent to *The Times* to Newman's great confusion. Ullathorne put the matter right. All that Newman asked was to be excused residence in Rome. In his letter of apology to Newman, Manning wrote (March 8, 1879): ' I fully believed that, for the reasons given in your letter, you declined what might be offered . . . if I misunderstood your intention it was by an error which I repaired the instant I knew it.' This has not been the view taken by historians who consider Manning really tried to suppress Newman's last noble ambition. Friends of both would prefer to believe that Manning had promoted Newman's Cardinalate from the beginning but there can be no doubt that Norfolk and Ripon in approaching him realized that it needed considerable presence of mind on his part to accept their suggestion. Once the suggestion was started Manning could not interpose but it was a relief to him when Newman appeared to decline the honour, and that relief he must have clinched by passing a secret to *The Times*.

Newman's great sensitiveness made him feel that Manning was standing in the way. He realized that what had been in the way more than anything was the Liberalism which was imputed to him and this he took pains to dissociate from his philosophy in his speech in Rome. This was particularly pleasing to the group attached to Manning. Herbert Vaughan, who echoed Manning's anti-Newmanism, wrote to Lady Herbert of Lea to say: ' He has done it with his own peculiar skill and pointedness. Nothing could have been more opportune or more forcible than his remarks about Liberalism,' and he reported that Manning had invited him to hold a reception in his house on his return from Rome. Newman preferred to hold it at Norfolk House where he felt more at home than under the roof of his brother in the sublime dignity.

If style is a guidance to the temperament or even to the character, how deeply the two Cardinals differed with the pen. Manning showed how ably he could have drawn up a political précis or an Act of Parliament, whereas Newman would have left such a document deliciously vague and allusive. Manning's style showed itself in drawing up diocesan plans, fighting an ecclesiastical case at Rome, imposing his views on fellow-bishops or in debating a dogma before a Council of the Church. His dry arid Parliamentary style won him a tremendous victory at Rome although he was not a deep theologian or a historian. It was the historians who nettled him and indeed made the opposition during the Council. Newman was a historian and understood the running fire of difficulties which men like Lord Acton could suggest. To Manning Acton was merely the malevolent counsellor of the bishops. Fortunately he did not come into collision or even contact with Newman during those wonderful months at Rome. He realized that the piercing letter in which Newman attacked ' an aggressive and insolent faction ' was perfectly private and should never have been revealed.

Newman's writings have remained as widely read as they were at publication. Manning's never had much longer life than his Pastorals. The *Eternal Priesthood* was the nearest he wrote to a classic. Much of what Newman wrote seems likely to endure as long as the language. Manning and his friends had little appreciation for a book like the *Apologia* which he curtly described as ' a voice from the dead.' For him the history of a spent Movement was behind him and he was only interested in the works of the immediate present. Oxford he had put behind him and trampled on her memory, whereas Newman clung to her enchantments all his life. His sensitive affection dwelt amongst her spires and his melancholy was soothed by the rocking of her bells.

To Manning Newman's novel *Callista* was ' coldly intellectual ' in comparison with Cardinal Wiseman's *Fabiola* which he found ' full of warmth and feeling.' The two phrases might also be used to describe their very different attitudes on the drink question. Manning showed the warmest feeling possible against alcohol in private or public life, whereas Newman might be said to take the ' coldly intellectual '

or sober liberal view that wine was made for the use (though
not for the abuse) of man. In his latter days when he had
exchanged dogmatic for social controversies Manning took a
stronger line against stimulants than any bishop before or
since. It will be remembered that he refused to allow his
life to be prolonged by their application. It can be said that
he was influenced not only by the drunkenness which was then
rife amongst the hard-working Irish labourers in England but
by some tragic episodes in his own family.

In his tremendous social reforming zeals, which really made
him a public character, Manning brought that obstinacy of
will power against which Newman and Newman's friends had
so often struggled in vain. Manning had a one track mind,
though he set it on several different tracks. Once he had set
his intellectual engine into action he followed the track
without stoppage and without turning into sidings. Newman
was intellectually more interested in side-issues than the main
line. Manning thought only of reaching his terminus at full
speed while Newman seemed to him playing with terms.
But Newman appealed to thousands of English minds which
had no desire to be rushed to Manning's conclusions whether
affecting the Temporal Power of the Holy See, the Catholic
Question in English Universities or indeed the Infallibility.

The Temporal Power (now quenched as a controversy in
the Lateran Treaty) was an aching one amongst Catholics
under *Pio Nono*. For Manning it was the keystone of the
Arch of Christendom. Newman was unwilling to give his
name to the newly formed *accademia* if the Temporal Power was
to be made an important ideal under Wiseman. In the end it
was the only big controversy on which Manning changed
views. In the end he decided that Providence had placed the
Italians in Rome! But in the controversial days he was inclined
to label all who opposed him amongst the English Catholics
as anti-Roman, Low Church, minimizers and disloyal to the
Holy See. It is indubitable that he included Newman in that
category. This was largely due to the pressing influence of
Ward who had better be described as Manning's theological
evil genius. Manning at one time seemed to allow the scheme
for sending Newman to Oxford until Ward asserted his
fanaticism. All that Manning conceived personally for the

good of the Church was attributed to the inspiration of the Holy Ghost. It might be said that Manning brought the devotion to the Third most Holy Person with him out of the old Evangelical circles of youth. He attributed his conversion to the same and indeed all the policies which he imposed upon the English Catholics. Many no doubt considered them no less inspired but the Newmanites found many of them an affliction. It seems a distant time when all converts in England arrived labelled as it seemed with the first query and answer of the Anglican Catechism—

' What is thy name?'
' N. or M.'

This was generally interpreted: Newmanite or Manningite. It was unfortunate that old Anglican rivalries and conflicts took a new lease on Catholic soil: but so it was and to understand the inner history of the Church in England for thirty years it is necessary to know the personalities involved. On the great scale, in their standing amongst the great Victorians, Manning and Newman equally adorned Church and State. It was the fault of their followers that their names were used to label and emblazon much that was petty and much that has since been discarded or settled by the Church. The Holy See regarded the English Catholics of that period as particularly quarrelsome!

Nothing was more admirable than the temper of the Holy See during all the troubles which seemed to distract English Catholicism. In the century which followed the restoration of the Hierarchy troubles hardly seemed to cease. Wiseman was fighting with his bishops in the Courts of Rome but in spite of the diplomatic influences brought to bear by Manning and Talbot, Wiseman steadily lost his case. The Holy See acting with immeasurable patience and a judicial fairness born of the ages refused to be carried away by the importunity of converts. There is what can be described as the pontifical pendulum and, though an apparent injustice or over-expressed policy may dominate during one Pope's reign, it is certainly straightened in the next. The attitude of Manning towards Newman was certainly reflected in Pius IX but the feelings

of the English Catholics as a whole found an interpreter in
Leo XIII. When he awarded the Red Hat to the saintly
Oratorian a wave of delight passed through Catholic and
Anglican ranks: it must be admitted surpassing the pleasure
shown four years previously at Manning's elevation. Lytton
Strachey in *Eminent Victorians* has endeavoured to make
Manning appear as actually thwarting Newman's honour.
Once admitted that he neither initiated nor approved of a
Hat which aureoled all that he had opposed in English Catholic
thought, Manning could claim to have furthered the project
once set forth by others. It should be remembered that his
own Hat had been long delayed. In fact he reigned for ten
years as Archbishop of Westminster without the coveted *rubra
galera*, as the language of the Church expresses it. No
biographer has been able to explain the reason of the long
delay except that the controversies at the Vatican Council
left him with some strong opponents in Church and Curia.
It was felt that for his position and standing he had exceeded
himself. There can be no doubt that he largely led and inspired the advanced Ultramontanes and came under the dis-
approval and suspicion of the Gallicans and Inopportunists.
No doubt if his Hat had been awarded in 1871 it would have
been regarded as an encouragement of ecclesiastical politics
and for this reason the Church has often omitted the most
brilliant and famous, because they inevitably become the most
controversial, from the ranks of the Sacred College. We recall
such names as Bishop Dupanloup and Archbishop Ireland.

It was as a Diocesan Bishop that Manning received his
reward. He had achieved a work which would have been
impossible for Newman in facing the rough and tumble of
public life. He forced the Catholic view into national
prominence. He cultivated statesmen and abashed scientists
to their face. Newman was shocked on hearing that Manning
had joined the Metaphysical Society and listened to Huxley
reading a Paper on the Resurrection. The Metaphysical was
the Brains Trust of Victorian days.

Who is capable of summing up these days as between
Manning and Newman? As Cardinal Barnabò once said:
' Manning I know but Newman I love.' Perhaps the sincerest
and best attempt occurs in the Essays of Father Dudley Ryder,

a nephew of Manning and an Oratorian of Newman. He compared them in their differences of psychology and attitude to ' the sea and the rocks confronting it.' No doubt Manning always acted and stood out as though he were part of the Rock of Peter. Newman in his moods of thought and music of language was as variable as the Ocean. But so they were both fashioned by their Creator and there we may leave them.

VI

MANNING AND THE VATICAN COUNCIL

By William Purdy

'Come again: it does me good to talk about it. It makes me live in the past.' Thus Manning ushered Wilfrid Ward out of Archbishop's House after a talk on the Vatican Council on an evening in 1891. Just a quarter of a century earlier Ward's father, Ideal Ward, or as some called him, Damnation Ward, had dedicated his *Authority of Doctrinal Decisions* to Manning with these words: 'There is nothing you have more earnestly taught us than that the interests of truth come before those of peace.' It was in the year following that dedication that Manning knelt with his friend the Bishop of Ratisbon at the tomb of St. Peter and vowed to do all in his power to obtain the definition of Papal Infallibility. In the medieval phrase, he took the cross, and might well have inscribed Ward's maxim on his banner.

It would be wrong to suppose that those who in this matter called themselves Inopportunists held the reverse maxim. Many of them thought that the interests of peace might justifiably delay the solemn definition of truth, but many of them were Inopportunists for a deeper reason: they were afraid, as Abbot Butler says, of the kind of Infallibility that might be defined.[1] They trembled at the thought of the New Ultramontanism being erected into a dogma. No such fears disturbed Manning or his theological second at Old Hall. Yet it would be a gross misconception of Manning to suppose him a Neo-Ultramontane merely because it was the most belligerent position he could hold. His belligerence was as exalted as his singlemindedness was intense. 'The dominant influence in his life,' said the younger Ward, 'was the power of conviction that certain lines of policy were entrusted to him by Providence to carry out against all human wills as part of

---

[1] Strictly of course it is nonsense to speak of being afraid of what might be defined; but the prevalence of particular opinions or tendencies might well make for nervousness in those who had the heavy responsibility of taking part in a General Council.

the great battle for the Church against the World, which he pictured in almost apocalyptic terms.' This has been the motive force of so many great authoritarians, ecclesiastical especially—the ability without pride or humbug to identify themselves with Destiny. The same strength and the same extravagance that drove the Old Hall divines to Hammersmith and set up the expensive toy university in Kensington were deployed in the van of the Infallibilist campaign. It was one of the glories of the Council that the strength was allowed full scope and the extravagance gently smothered. With Manning, as with so many before and after him, Rome was *patiens quia aeterna*.

Summing up on the Great Definition, the hostile Pomponio Leto says: ' All know that it was their mind and will that carried it '—meaning Manning and the fathers of the *Civiltà Cattolica*. Whatever part Manning's will may have played, what was defined was much nearer to Bellarmine's mind, or even to Newman's, than to Manning's or Ward's. Manning has often been compared with Gladstone, whom Bagehot described as ' a second-class brain in a first-class state of fermentation.' The ferment of Manning's brain in the Rome of the Council helped, in its way, to produce a wine of doctrine that Bellarmine and Fénelon would have savoured better than Veuillot or Ward.

Fénelon was in the strict sense the first Ultramontane, though Bellarmine was the classical exponent of the doctrine long before the name was thought of. There is no mystery about it—it can be found in any good treatise *De Ecclesia*. The student, reading it in that historical vacuum, finds it hard to discover any patience for those who in the Council resisted to the last ditch and finally left Rome on the morning of July 18, 1870, rather than vote *non placet*. To understand these bishops—nearly all of them great apostolic men—one must understand the half-century of turmoil—intellectual, social, political—through which they had lived. The New Ultramontanism generated out of that turmoil, far from being definable was not a theological doctrine at all in the respectable sense. Its father was the man of affairs, de Maistre, and over it as over him hung the shadow of the Revolution. Behind his *Du Pape* was the ' vision of horror of '93,' a vision penetrating far beneath the spectacular horror of the guillotine to the cankered roots of society. He saw in an infallible Pope a last stronghold of authority and stability amid an apocalypse of ruin. It is hard to make sense of the growth of the New Ultramontanism apart from this sense of an ancient civilization overturned—this loathing of the ideas and deeds of '93. *La Revolution est un œuvre Français, donc un œuvre exageré*, said de Maistre: the New Ultramontanism too was precisely that.

Curiously, it shared with its antagonist, Catholic Liberalism, a common ancestry. With de Lamennais the universal consent is the test of truth, and its mouthpiece is the infallible Pope, to whom no one can deny even the deposing power without separation from God. It is hardly credible that in 1842 Montalembert wrote of Veuillot: 'He has ravished me: there is a man after my own heart.' But so it is. They split over the Falloux education bill in 1850, the liberals took the path that foreshadowed Leo XIII's *ralliement* and Veuillot with his *Univers* flew off on the career of intransigent extravagance that culminated, on the eve of the Council, in the frightful parody of the nones hymn

Rerum PIUS tenax vigor. . . .

The prize for this sort of frolic was carried off by Gaume, who wrote a four-hundred-page treatise on Holy Water, traced all the evils of the age to the study of the classics and dismissed Aristotle as the father of atheistic materialism. It is hard for us after two generations of security and calm under the *Constitutio de Fide Catholica* to realize the scandal, the damage and disturbance, the intemperate retaliation caused by all this untheological and unhistorical froth. It is against such a background that the famous and disastrous letter of Newman to Ullathorne must be seen. The truth is that many even among genuine Ultramontanes were terrified of the Great Question being aired in such an atmosphere.

For some years before the Council Veuillot's paper *L'Univers* carried on warfare against the French bishops. This warfare dated indeed from Gallican days, but as its original cause waned its intensity waxed. ' I have no influence with my clergy,' said Cardinal Mathieu, ' the *Univers* is all-powerful with them.' Papal pronouncements addressed to bishops in technical language and requiring a background for their full understanding reached the laity direct through the *Univers*, with the latter's interpretation on them. The worst case was that of the great Syllabus of 1864—perhaps the classical exposure of fashionable progressive nonsense, but needing careful reading and interpretation especially in one or two of the more compressed or more allusive condemned propositions. It was travestied in the French anti-clerical press (one paper, for example, translated the heading ' *Errores de Societate Civili* ' as ' Errors of Civil Society ') but none travestied it more heartily than the New Ultramontanes. When it is remembered that Veuillot had written as early as 1852, ' It has been said that the Parliamentary system rests on an heretical principle: whatever desire we have to avoid exaggeration, we think that this is not to say enough,' it can easily be imagined how he manhandled the syllabus. But he was surpassed again by Gaume, who in a cheap pamphlet boiling down the Syllabus unpardonably insinuated an attack on Montalembert and his friends, classing them with the Jansenists.

It was not necessary to be a contributor to the *Rambler* or even a Newman or Dupanloup to feel uneasy about all this, and of course it played into the hands of the extreme liberal left. Over-simplification was then as now the life-blood of leftism, and the intransigents were generous blood-donors. French Inopportunism, in fact, was far less a relic of Gallicanism than a reaction against the *Univers*.

In England the chief exponent of the New Ultramontanism was W. G. Ward, the lay professor of theology at Old Hall. As a good theologian he was fortified against most of the excesses above referred to. ' *Sentire cum ecclesia* ' was his excellent watchword, which meant, he contended, the fullest acceptance of Papal pronouncements by the people straight from the Pope and never mind the professors. A clever specialist, he said, could drive a coach and four through a papal utterance. Not being a reader of the *Univers*, he failed perhaps fully to grasp what an equally clever and more intemperate journalist could do with it. He ended by maintaining that not only was the Syllabus infallible *in toto* but so were all the sources from which it drew.

As with the French intransigents, much that is most startling in Ward must be put down to polemical repulsion. He shared with his Archbishop a robust aversion to current liberalizing, to ' clever devils,' and their common *bête noire* was the *Rambler*.[1] (It is a pretty irony that in 1858 Acton wrote of Manning as one of the bright prospects for his journal.) This was no surface irritation—it was rooted in profound convictions and a profound mistrust. To Ward and Manning, as to such a very different man as John Morley, the real division of the time was between Christianity and the Revolution, and those who suffered from intellectual pride were, to Ward and Manning, the natural allies of the latter force, whatever their professions of loyalty. (The trouble of course is that if you hold this view of intellectual pride you must be very careful in deciding who suffers from it.) De Maistre had invited men to come in under the shadow of the Rock in the Waste Land of Jacobinism; to Ward and Manning the mental Waste Land represented by Comte's Positivism and Strauss' *Life of Jesus* was quite as real, and they sought the same shelter. ' An internecine conflict is at hand between the army of dogma and the united hosts of indifferentism, heresy and atheism,' wrote Manning. It was in this state of martial exaltation that he marched to the lists in the cause of Ultramontanism, and woe to anyone who was careless enough to be found even dallying on the fringes of the ' united hosts ' of the opposition. A Lacordaire, a Dupanloup, an Ozanam, a Newman did not avail to fumigate the haunts of Liberal Catholicism. ' Illness is catching—health is not,' said Ward firmly. It remained to close the ranks—to forge links with continental Ultramontanism for the battle ahead.

Manning never lacked the power of restraint, as his pastorals are enough to show. He induced Ward to withdraw his essay on liberty of conscience, aimed against Montalembert, for fear of giving offence. Other letters to Ward show a healthy contrast to the vicarious infallibility assumed by the *Univers*. This said, it remains a valid criticism that he never sufficiently dissociated himself from the wilder extravagances of the New Ultramontanism. He worked hard and often suppressed himself to preserve unity at home, but the crusading temper in which he approached the Infallibility question reinforced a natural aversion to nuances: one was either an Ultramontane

---

[1] There are volumes of historical commentary in Simpson's schoolboyish remark to Ward: ' Come for a walk with me, and I will make your hair stand on end.'

or anti-Roman and a worldly Catholic. His deep mistrust of the old Catholics and of Newman, constantly fanned by the egregious Monsignor Talbot (and, it must fairly be admitted, rarely aired with complete candour except to that dignitary), too often inclined him to heresy-hunting. Happily, the very nature of his zeal carried with it its own corrective. What he preached to others—complete and prompt submission to the Pope—he was always ready to practise. Ward's theses were submitted to Rome, only very partially endorsed and considerably modified long before the Council. All Manning's feelings and convictions inclined him to hope and press for the most comprehensive definition possible of Infallibility; but by the same token, Dupanloup's words to Veuillot, ' I reproach you with making the Church participate in your violences by giving as its doctrines, with rare audacity, your most personal ideas,' could hardly in the fiercest heat have been applied to Manning. ' So long as I know that I have only repeated the words of the Holy See I have no anxiety,' he wrote—though it will be seen that he had no objection to prompting the Holy See as much as possible.

A Roman damper was placed on his exuberance at the Public Consistory which proclaimed the Council in 1867. He was present at the drawing-up of the bishops' congratulatory address replying to the allocution, and advocated a fighting manifesto, ' wounding in order to strike home.' The presiding Cardinal imposed moderation: there was no need to *make* trouble in France and Italy; and the Bishop of Grenoble, furious with Manning, said fiercely to Ullathorne, ' *Ce n'est pas le temps de casser les vitraux.*'

The drafting was eventually consigned to a committee on which, ironically, Manning found himself with Haynald and Dupanloup, two leading Inopportunists. In the first draft the word ' infallible ' appeared four times; in the final draft, to Manning's disappointment, it did not appear at all, but by sheer insistence he got inserted the Florentine decree on the Primacy. This involved him in a very sharp encounter with Dupanloup—to which, according to Ullathorne, Pius IX prompted him. In spite of this, Manning pays generous tribute to Dupanloup: ' He is a vigorous man, and the more I see of him the more I like him. He has the heart of a

G

pastor.' The more pity that the *Tablet* should have been allowed to exhibit such shocking manners towards him.

The two years that separated this meeting from the assembling of the Council were unfortunately full of events unlikely to sweeten the atmosphere. In France Maret, dean of the theological faculty at the Sorbonne and one of the few surviving genuine Gallicans, published a two-volume manifesto, which was followed a month later by that of the Catholic Liberals—an article entitled *Le Concile* in the *Correspondant*. It is difficult today either to convey or to understand the fury aroused on the French ' right ' by this, but unless the deep and bitter divisions in French life and thought are appreciated it is quite impossible to understand the Inopportunism of French bishops at all. Much ignorant comment at the time attributed it to Gallicanism. Manning himself, scarcely a minimizer of unorthodox tendencies, admitted that not half-a-dozen French bishops showed any trace of Gallican ideas.

Dupanloup of Orleans issued a very correct and uncontroversial pastoral, but followed it by a letter to his clergy which is a representative statement of the Inopportunist position. As an *ad clerum* this was perhaps unexceptionable. There was nothing heretical about inopportunism—nothing even *piarum aurium offensivum* unless one interprets *pius* in a very narrow sense. It was a pity that Dupanloup saw fit to add here what would, separately published, have been excellent and opportune—a sharp criticism of the antics of the *Univers*. This brought him down into the arena with a crash that echoed as far as the Vatican. Pius IX, who owed a tremendous debt to Dupanloup, kept his head and spoke the bishop fair, which regrettably was a good deal more than could be said for the *Tablet*; it leapt into the argument with large and disastrous feet.

In Germany the prelude to the Council was even more unhappy. The one-time champion of the Church, Döllinger, had for some time been growing in antagonism to the Papacy, and an extravagant report in the *Civiltá Cattolica* of February 1869 alleging that there was a strong French movement for defining Infallibility by acclamation, led him to take the lead in the notorious series of articles which later appeared in book form as *Janus*. This pernicious book, which represented the most extreme theories of the *Univers* type as doctrines of the Church and ridiculed them with great weight of learning, caused a violent eruption in Germany. (Among others it attacked Manning and pronounced, wrongly as the event proved: ' the English bishops will all follow him.') The Catholic bishops and lay leaders kept their heads well, but many of them were made Inopportunists. Again this can only be understood in relation to the prevailing atmosphere, the best parallel for which in history would seem to be that of fourth-century Byzantium, where a man could not get his hair cut without risk of losing blood in a theological brawl. When a Catholic champion so intrepid as Von Ketteler was Inopportunist it was absurd to treat the viewpoint as other than respectable.

It was in this atmosphere that Manning entered the lists. Whether or not he admitted a need for caution or delicacy, he certainly achieved none. One suspects that he had little real grasp of the complex and inflammable continental situation, and that he cared little anyway now that he smelt the battle afar off. He very fortunately sent his Letter on Infallibility to Ullathorne before publishing it. Ullathorne was horrified. ' It would have put France in a fury,' he wrote later—and recommended sending it to the chief theologian at Maynooth, who watered it down considerably, with the droll result that it was praised by *The Times* and other English papers for its ' straightforwardness '! A hasty postscript added on receipt of Maret's book brought him into collision with Dupanloup, but it was a minor dispute.

Manning was not the intellectual leader of the Infallibilist party—he has been aptly called its Chief Whip. His persuasions were always of a practical order: the definition was opportune because it would consolidate authority in the face of the Revolution. It almost seemed that, if men were Inopportunists out of timidity, Manning aspired to make them Infallibilists by scaring them more profoundly. An account of his impact was given to Purcell in conversation by Moufang, theologian to Von Ketteler:

Archbishop Manning, by his vehement and vivid forecasts of the evils which threatened us, made my hair stand on end. But there was a great deal of force in his arguments. Our opposition to the opportuneness of the Definition was confined more or less to historical or theoretical objections; we gave little or no thought to the practical view of things which Manning insisted upon; to the coming events in the political order, wars and revolutions which he predicted with such terrible earnestness. We were, perhaps, more of theologians; he more of an ecclesiastical statesman.

Theological discussion proper, at a deep and valuable level, was carried on between the two parties, e.g., between Dupanloup and Dechamps of Malines. This needs stressing—it is easy to lose sight of it and get the impression that all extra-conciliar activity was of a backstairs kind. Infallibility was not defined over the cups of tea dispensed by those whom Veuillot christened the *commeres du Concile*; but the vehemence and excited language of the protagonists themselves probably gave an inflated idea of the importance of this running back and forth in the Roman heat.

Much more serious was the diplomatic activity properly so called that the Council stimulated. It was directed almost entirely against the Ultramontane party, and was first aroused (again, inexplicably apart from the hysterical state of opinion at the time) by the very moderate propositions in the *Schema* that touched on Church and State. This activity centred chiefly around Döllinger, who was not only influential at the Bavarian court but was a friend of Acton and Gladstone; but it was also found in France. It did more than anything to taint the opposition to the Definition. Its moving spirits formed themselves into an international committee, against which stood a similar caucus for the Definition; in this of course Manning was at the forefront. He writes:

> We met at my rooms, at Ratisbon's and Paderborn's rooms, and finally at the Villa Caserta. One day the opposition came and half filled the room. We had to adjourn. The international committee met often, and we met weekly to watch and counteract. When they went to Pius IX, we went also. It was a running fight.

The first victory in the running fight was to get the *Deputatio de Fide* formed entirely of Infallibilists. There is no point in

trying to improve on Butler's judgement of this, and the scope
of this chapter demands that the passage be quoted fully:

After going through the proceedings of the entire Council,
I have to say that this appears to me as the one serious blot
on its doings. It was surely an error of judgement not to
accord to a considerable and influential minority, counting
among its members a number of the foremost and most
justly respected bishops of the Church, some representation,
some vehicle for the expression of its views on this committee. The practical effect was that the minority became
an Opposition, exasperated by the sense that the Majority
was bent on overwhelming it by mere force of numbers,
without giving it a fair hearing. And it afforded to the
enemies of the Council outside one of their most effective
weapons in inveighing against the lack of real freedom of the
bishops, contending that the appearance of election was
camouflage, everything being engineered by the Curia.
Some of the bishops felt the like. . . .
For this proceeding it seems that Manning has to take the
responsibility. It was not in accordance with the Pope's
wish . . . it was his expressed wish that representatives
of the Minority, and Dupanloup by name, should be on the
deputation *de Fide*, in order that the Minority might not
feel aggrieved at having no advocate on it. The same was
urged at the preliminary meeting by the Latin Patriarch
of Jerusalem and Cardinal Corsi, both of the Majority.
But Manning was inflexible. As a contemporary letter
had it, perhaps ironically: ' The humble convert, Mgr
Manning, resisted the proposal and brought about its
abandonment.' ' See,' says Granderath (the classical historian of the Council), ' on the one side the Pope, the Patriarch
and Cardinal Corsi; and on the other a simple member of
the Council, Mgr Manning. . . .' One cannot but think
it regrettable that Manning's Ultramontane principle
sentire cum Papa did not on this occasion make him bow to
the Pope's wish; but ' heretics,' he said, ' come to a Council
to be heard and condemned, not to take part in formulating
doctrine.' It seems that the Pope was somewhat disturbed
at this intransigent action and we know that Pie of Poitiers,
leading Ultramontane though he was and himself second
in the poll, disapproved of the whole proceeding, comparing
the tactics to the official candidatures of governments and
municipalities, and saying he had no part in it.

The English bishops, of whom so far only four took sides—
two with Manning and two with the Minority—put forward
the moderate Ultramontane Grant as their representative—
' to the Archbishop's surprise, evinced by sundry snortings and
extra politeness,' wrote Ullathorne; but it was Manning who
was elected.

This was on December 20, 1869. During the next few
days the Infallibilist G.H.Q. prepared a circular to the bishops
promoting a petition for the Definition. It should be remembered of course that the latter was not yet formally a part of
the Council's ' agenda.' This consisted primarily of four or
five great general *schemata* prepared by commissions of experts,
which would be subject to discussion in public session and
referable if found unsatisfactory to their appropriate deputation
or committee. For the rest the right of proposing particular
subjects was vested in the Pope, though bishops could make
suggestions in writing to a congregation, *de Postulatis*, set up
for the purpose.

The Infallibilist petition was at first circulated secretly,
afterwards openly. Some of the English bishops saw it first
in the papers, and Manning later told Ullathorne that he had
kept it from them ' out of delicacy.'[1] The Minority of course
raised counter-petitions, but Pius IX quite properly refused
to receive personally any of these instruments. It is note-
worthy that in the face of all this many of the bishops consistently refused to have anything to do with extra-Conciliar
movements—notably Ullathorne and Pie. The word
' intrigue ' was freely tossed about: just as a tripper is any
tourist except oneself, so intrigue is any diplomacy except one's
own. To maintain neutrality and independence in this
atmosphere required courage and dexterity of a high order.

' You will find the Holy Ghost inside the Council, not
outside of it,' Pius IX used to say to audiences. It is a refreshment to turn from this atmosphere of canvass, contrivance and
too free counter-accusation to the inside of the Council. The
first debate on the *schema de Fide* struck a rousing note of

---

[1] Mention of petitions recalls the amusing story of Manning suggesting to
Rymer, the President of St. Edmund's, that the boys in the school should sign
a petition for the Definition. The respectful reply was that the little boys
were part of the *ecclesia discens*, and it would be most unsuitable for them to
presume to prompt bishops and theologians.

vigorous candour which persisted to the end. The first speech of the Vatican Council was made by the Cardinal of Vienna; he roundly rated the *schema* as long, vague and academic. The Bishop of Halifax, Nova Scotia, said it tried to treat ' *de omni scibili in re dogmatica,*' and would make the Fathers of Trent turn in their graves. The great Ballerini later gave academic support to this criticism, describing the work of his fellow-Jesuits as ' *moles indigesta, opus de novo conficiendum.*' It was in fact sent back for that purpose to the *deputatio de Fide,* 'mangled and pulled to pieces, bleeding in every limb,' in Ullathorne's words.

Nor did the Right Reverend Fathers confine themselves to criticizing *schemata.* They were strongly appreciative of fine speeches, of which there were plenty, but when after several long and tedious ones a bishop mounted the pulpit and said he would only keep them a quarter of an hour there were loud cries of ' *bene, optime.*' There was little fear from the start that the freedom of the Council would be affected by any of the influences at work outside.

Many will agree with Abbot Butler in regretting that the world was not able from the start to learn fully of this healthy and imposing atmosphere, instead of hearing only the reports of extra-Conciliar manoeuvres and the lush imaginings of the pressmen and touts of every sort who hung about the entrance to the screened-off south transept of St. Peter's. The *Times* correspondent, one Mozley, in particular was an inexhaustible fountain of good clean fun. The secrecy imposed under oath was impossible to keep and was in fact very badly kept. Manning was dispensed from it in order to enable Russell, the British Government's agent (himself no model of discretion), to counter the reports sent by Acton to Gladstone. But in fact the violently hostile reports circulated by the Döllinger faction could have no adequate refutation while secrecy was imposed. It was certainly a pity that Acton dispensed himself so liberally from the austere standards of accuracy and impartiality he was to set to youthful historians at Cambridge. While Manning was in no position to be censorious about ' the baseness of the partisan spirit, the parliamentary whipping and canvassing and intrigue,' as he was in the rather churlish reminiscences of 1887, he was justified in complaining to

Gladstone (April 1870) that the latter ' was hearing only one side, and that from a partisan (Acton) of the most hostile animus.' This could not have been, had full official reports been available.

While the press fabricated stories of disorder and lack of free speech, the Fathers themselves during a long break in February and March robustly advanced exactly contrary criticism, even to the Pope himself. There was too much rhetoric: the general feeling was wittily summed up '*per totam noctem laborantes nihil cepimus.*' The criticisms received acknowledgement in a number of supplementary regulations for procedure when sessions were resumed.

Meantime the petitions laid before the congregation *de Postulatis* resulted at last in that body recommending, with only one dissentient voice (Rauscher of Vienna), that the Great Question be brought before the Council. The public announcement of this (March 6, 1870) was the second Infallibilist triumph, and a critical phase of the Council. There was some feverish diplomatic activity, and for a month the danger of political intervention hung over the Council. To this time belongs what was perhaps Manning's most valuable service— his co-operation with Odo Russell in averting the intervention of the British government, which Acton had been pressing upon Gladstone with all his might. There existed between Manning and Gladstone that coolness which is only found between once close friends who have parted on some deep issue, but Manning's letter of April 6 is a moderate and firm one: the remark concerning Acton has already been quoted, and the letter goes on:

For the sake of us all, for your own sake, for your future, for the peace of our country, do not allow yourself to be warped, or impelled into words or acts hostile to the Council. If you desire to do good to Ireland and therefore to the empire, do not render it impossible by touching a religious question.

The French ministry, with great imprudence, or at least some members of it, have attempted, and may attempt again, to put pressure on the Council. I feel it to be a duty to say that in such an event we are prepared for the course we shall have to take. The question will be reduced to

the simplest terms, and our next step is inevitable. I wish
to say this beforehand. The repeated efforts of the Opposition here to invoke the interference of the Civil Governments
are well known to us. No such interference will have a
shadow's weight in the Council; but it will impose upon us
duties not free from many dangers, but to be done at the
cost of all things. I believe that you would wish me to be
perfectly open on such a subject.

The fears which move me to write may be groundless, and
then I hope you will excuse me having so written. But
there are great things at stake, and we are both responsible.

The announcement of March 6 naturally redoubled activity:
pamphlets poured, discussion and canvassing raged. A revival
of the cock-and-bull story about carrying the Definition by
acclamation increased tension—it seems to have been taken
surprisingly seriously by the Minority. A weighty pamphlet
by the great Von Ketteler of Mainz was deliberately held up
at the Post Office until representations were made to Antonelli.
It was this mounting tension that induced many bishops to
petition the President and finally the Pope himself to bring
on the Question out of its turn. Manning was of course well
to the fore. It was not unreasonably argued that to send the
bishops back to their sees now with the question undecided
would be to make intolerable difficulties for them. One
bishop said of the Minority: ' *quod inopportunum dixerunt
necessarium fecerunt.*' The Minority on the other hand saw
the move as an attempt ' to forestall the hour of Providence and
carry the thing by assault '; thus wrote Dupanloup to Pius IX,
and received a fatherly exhortation to be a little less obstinate.

The revised *schema* ' *de Romano Pontifice* ' was in fact tabled
on May 13, and the decisive debate on it, decisive because it
settled the question of ' opportuneness,' occupied the rest of
the month. On May 25 Manning had his great day: he
made his speech of one hour and fifty minutes before the
Council.

I wrote the whole by myself, and afterwards read it over
to Bishop Cornthwaite and Padre Liberatore. They made
no change in it. . . . Before I got up I was nervous, but
once up perfectly calm. I saw dear old Cardinal de Angelis
look in despair at the cardinals next to him, as if he thought I

should never end. But the bishops never moved till I had done. Cardinal Monaco, who was at the greatest distance, told me that he heard every word.

Thus he proudly recalled it in 1887, and rightly, for it was well received.

On June 3 the closure was applied. It caused much murmuring, but it was done at the express wish of a majority of bishops. None could deny that both sides of the question had been aired to the point of tedium. It was beginning to get very hot in Rome; the heat of the sun doubtless contributed to a cooling of the climate of opinion. By May 25 Ullathorne was writing of the attendance thinning, and adding: ' For a week past conferences have been going on . . . tending to an accommodation. I spoke to Malines this morning, who assured me that a plan was almost matured for an accord, and he told me some of the details. . . .'

Clifford was getting thin, and Manning solicitously asked him and Amherst (Northampton) whether they had not better go home. Both were Minority men !

The Definition debate proper began on June 15. It was most thoroughly prepared for. A draft decree had been sent out in March, and 140 sets of ' observations ' on it received, and since April 29 the bishops had had before them a synopsis of these running to a hundred folio columns.

The principal question now remaining was that of the form the definition should take, and it gave scope for much variety of opinion.

The sensation of the debate was the Archbishop of Bologna's speech, which showed considerable and unexpected sympathy with the minority point of view. He was called over the coals on the same evening by Pius IX, argued that he had only said ' the bishops are the witnesses of tradition,' and received the famous reply: ' La tradizione son' io.' Nevertheless his speech greatly furthered rapprochement between the contending parties.

It may be surmised that from this point onwards such pacific overtures were of greater moment than the debate itself, which became more wearisome and repetitious as the thermometer mounted. The only purpose that was now being served was to kill any possible reproach of inadequate discussion or restraint of freedom of expression. The trend towards accommodation which had been going on since the draft decree had come before the deputation *de Fide* was resisted every inch of the way by the lean angel of Westminster. But the technique of the Chief Whip was not perhaps completely successful at deputation meetings. ' *Non ita sunt tractandae res ecclesiae,*' said Cardinal Bilio sternly on one occasion. It may have been ' no time for rose-water ' in writing in the *Tablet,* but the opinions of bishops who were also renowned scholars were, even if at last rejected, entitled to that full consideration which to Manning appeared only as a confession of weakness.

In the event such modifications as were made were insufficient to reduce substantially the Minority,[1] who were divided only on the question of procedure. It was Dupanloup's influence that at last prevailed in favour of abstention from voting at the final session, to prevent possible scandal in the Catholic world.

There were consequently only two *non placets* on the historic morning of July 18 when, to the accompaniment of thunder and lightning, in a scene racily described by the inimitable Mozley and doubtless deeply relished by the ex-archdeacon of Chichester, the Roman Pontiff was declared infallible. Those two intrepid dissidents deserve their peculiar immortality; their names evoke catholicity of time and space: Fitzgerald of Little Rock, U.S.A. and Riccio of Cajazzo in the Kingdom of Naples. The moment the Pope had confirmed the Constitution both of them came down and knelt humbly at his feet. ' *Modo credo, sancte Pater,*' said the Irish Yankee; ' *Credo,*' echoed the heir of Greeks, Arabs and Normans. And perhaps the facial muscles of the onetime captain of Harrow softened for a moment.

On the next day war was declared between France and Prussia, and exactly two months later the Piedmontese, and so much else besides, entered the City. Canon Moufang's hair had not stood vainly on end.

' As a private theologian,' Abbot Butler has said, ' Pius IX was a pronounced Neo-Ultramontane.' As the Council wore

---

[1] These were notable ' converts '—The Primate of Germany and the Archbishops of New York, Avignon, Rheims and Sens.

on he was less and less at pains to conceal his private views—views which the Council certainly did not define any more than it defined those of Manning or Ward. Pius was loved and venerated to a remarkable degree by all, and not the least of the trials of those who felt bound to opposition was the thought of offending him and incurring his displeasure. The Archbishop of Westminster was spared such trials, and it may be questioned how far he even understood the hesitations of a scholar like Hefele or the difficulties weighing on a man like Strossmayer who ruled a diocese on the confines of the Latin West.

' Until I had attended one myself,' wrote Manning seventeen years later, ' I had never understood aright the history of the Councils. I now understand how Councils were delayed or broken up or intimidated. I can put my finger by the light of the present on the culprits of the past.' What Manning in fact seems to do in these reminiscences is rather the opposite—to dramatize the Vatican Council in terms of the more sensational aspects of Nicaea and Constantinople. It is arguable, however (though by no means made clear), that his strictures refer to the Döllinger party, which contained so many people he personally disliked. In any case some allowance must be made for the crustiness of old age. It remains a pity that such a landmark in the history of dogma should seem to be relished chiefly as the discomfiture of personal opponents. Whatever may be the truth about Ephesus or Chalcedon (and only the inflated historian pretends wholly to know) it is surely reasonable to argue that the great definition hammered out in the Roman heat of 1870 was as much the reward of the labours of the Minority fathers as of the zelantes, and not the epic triumph of the emissaries of light over the children of darkness.

Manning often seemed to use action too complex to further what he conceived in terms too simple; but in a matter most complex to profound minds the only simple thing, simple and mysterious, was the action of the Holy Ghost, before which at last all bowed with Catholic docility. ' *Non in commotione Dominus*,' said the witty Pius IX as the storm died away and the Definition was done. Manning sometimes seemed too much to relish a commotion, but he too at his happiest and in other fields could judge and act ' in the spirit of a gentle air.'

VII

MANNING AND EDUCATION

By Christopher Howard

There are few fields of activity in which Manning's still numerous critics can find more occasions for adverse comment than that of education. All too often the Cardinal was guilty of discouraging the sincere efforts of those within his jurisdiction, of failing to appreciate the needs of his time, of neglecting valuable potential allies and of misunderstanding the aims and capabilities of dangerous opponents. In assessing the value of Manning's work for education one cannot but recognize that the debit column is long and well-filled.

Fortunately, however, several of Manning's errors are so well known that there is no need to analyse them in detail. His biographers have already told us much of what we need to know about the fields of higher and secondary education, in which his most widely criticized decisions were made.

His attitude to the problem of university education revealed a failure to appreciate the attraction that the older English Universities held for young men of means—an attraction that was becoming all the greater with the gradual change in the character of Oxford and Cambridge. Less and less were they recruiting-grounds for the clergy of the Establishment; more and more, as a result of the expansion of governmental activity and the Order in Council of June 4, 1870 were they becoming schools for the various civil services, which now offered increasing opportunities of congenial, secure and comparatively well-paid employment; at the same time Cambridge in particular was rapidly developing its resources for the study of natural science. To the problem created by this situation Manning failed to provide a solution. His attempt to discourage Catholics from attending the older universities was only partially successful; the Catholic University College which he established in Kensington had to close its doors in 1878 after only four years of unhappy existence.

Nor was his work in the sphere of secondary education without blemish. Much that might have been accomplished was prevented by his dislike and distrust of the orders and congregations in whose hands the responsibility for secondary education largely lay, and in particular of the Society of Jesus. It is all too easy to point to opportunities for the loss of which Manning must bear at least a share of the blame.

It is clearly therefore neither in the sphere of higher nor in that of secondary education that any major and lasting achievement can be claimed on Manning's behalf. Such a claim, if made at all, can only be in respect of his work for primary education—one of the less, if not the least, known aspects of his archiepiscopate.

Manning's appointment to Westminster was made only two years before the Reform Act of 1867. The implications of that act were evident; they were tersely expressed by Robert Lowe. Successive censuses and the Newcastle Commission had shown that the existing schools, provided by voluntary effort supplemented by grants from the Privy Council, had not abolished illiteracy. The enfranchisement of a million new electors had therefore as its corollary new legislation to achieve that literate electorate without which representative government could not be workable.

The Reform Act was to be followed by a general election and the election would be followed at no great interval by an education bill. No great prescience was required to see that on the result of the election the character of that bill would depend. The Conservative Party was essentially the party of the Establishment, the Liberals an amalgam of Whigs and Radicals, the latter of whom were for the most part in sympathy with the programme of compulsory, gratuitous and unsectarian education which was shortly to be adopted by the Education League. The situation called for the most skilful diplomacy.

That Manning and the other members of the hierarchy realized that issues fundamental to the future of the Catholic schools were at stake in this period is beyond doubt. From Birmingham Ullathorne wrote to him (February 11, 1868): ' I altogether agree with you that the conscience clause, educational rate and compulsory education are the harbingers of a general system of education for this country which to us would be absolutely ruinous.'[1] But the ruinous implications of the Radical education policy were not brought home to the new voters. Instead, Gladstone dominated the election with his proposal to disestablish the Church of Ireland—a proposal which appealed strongly to both Irish Catholics and English Nonconformists—and other issues were swept aside. ' The Irish Bishops are persuaded,' Cardinal Cullen had written Manning from Dublin on April 8, 1867, ' that peace and love for authority can never be established in Ireland as long as the Catholics shall be obliged to support a Protestant establishment.' ' The main cause of all division, conflict and animosity is the Irish Establishment,' wrote Manning to his brother John on April 2, 1868 on the eve of the debate that led to the defeat of Disraeli's government. After the general election was over Archbishop Ullathorne wrote (November 20, 1868): ' Our elections in Birmingham were admirably managed, and with very good feeling towards us. Irishmen put on all the Liberal committees, half-hourly communications between all the eighty tolbooths. The English fraternized with the Irish. The priests were treated with marked respect.' The new Parliament saw an overwhelming Liberal majority with the Radical element stronger than ever before.

When, however, the expected education bill was introduced in the House of Commons on February 17, 1870, Manning, together with the entire hierarchy, was in Rome attending the Vatican Council. It passed through all its stages without his taking any step to protect the Catholic schools whose vital interests were so closely affected. Such modifications as were made in the bill during its passage through Parliament were concessions to the Radical members of the Liberal Party with their Nonconformist or secularist sympathies.

It is interesting to reflect what concessions Manning might have obtained. Much might have been gained, for the antidenominational ire of the Radicals and the Education League seems to have been directed against the schools of the Establishment rather than the far less numerous Catholic schools.

---

[1] The letter from which this passage is quoted is preserved among the papers of Cardinal Manning, for permission to use which I am deeply indebted to the Father Superior of the Oblates of St Charles. Unless otherwise stated, all other letters quoted in this article are from the same source.

Some sort of separate treatment for Catholic schools might have been achieved without great difficulty. As it was, the Catholic case went by default and Catholic schools received no special treatment. Catholics found themselves compelled to pay a local education rate from which their own schools drew not a penny, but which was spent solely on non-denominational schools established by the boards set up under the new statute. Manning's subsequent efforts in the field of primary education were to consist very largely of attempts to modify the settlement of 1870.

Not that the new Act represented a victory for Radicals and Nonconformists. It was a compromise with which no section of opinion was wholly satisfied. Nonconformist disappointment was at least as keen as Catholic and far more loudly expressed. John Bright, a moderate critic compared with some of his Birmingham constituents, wrote to Gladstone: ' The whole misfortune . ... has arisen from the error of making the new Act instrumental in preserving and extending indefinitely the system of " Denominational Schools "—a system bad from the beginning . . . instead of employing it to fill up the void which " Denominationalism " had left, in the hope that by and by all the schools of the Sects and Churches would merge into and become parts of the new system.'[1] That the settlement was a compromise, satisfying nobody and unlikely to prove lasting was the opinion also of Lord Salisbury, expressed in a letter to Manning of November 6, 1885. ' The Education Act of 1870 was a very clumsy compromise, intended rather to give time for the enemies of religious education to gather their strength than to effect any just and permanent settlement of the question. I earnestly hope that it will be possible to review the arrangement in a sense favourable to religious teaching.' Nor had Gladstone himself any enthusiasm for the 1870 settlement, despite the responsibility he bore for it. ' I wish,' runs an undated letter to Manning from Forster, ' you could have heard Gladstone's speech—the last half was very powerful and eloquent and went down to the roots of the question—but it was curious to see how his love of dogma peeped out: the same feeling which

---

[1] Trevelyan, *Life of John Bright*, p. 408.

makes him really prefer secular state teaching to the British and Foreign non-denominational system.'

Manning's correspondence with Salisbury and Forster is of particular interest as showing how after 1870 he sought a friendly understanding on the education question with members of both the principal political parties, including such a loyal supporter of the Establishment as Salisbury. Sir Charles Dilke, closely associated with the Education League, a reputed republican and with Positivist sympathies, was another whom Manning cultivated. All were valuable potential allies, as a letter from Manning to Ullathorne makes clear. ' I had on Friday a long and careful talk with Mr Forster,' he wrote on March 12, 1883. ' He will do us no harm; nor will he promote secular or free schools. He will say this when the subject comes up.' Forster was by no means the opponent of Church schools that he may at first sight have appeared.

It was not for several years after the passing of the 1870 Act that Manning took action to secure a new settlement. In 1882 and 1883 he published a series of four articles in *The Nineteenth Century* on the working of the 1870 Act, and in the following year was founded the Voluntary Schools Association to campaign for a more favourable settlement. It was the year of the third Reform Act and another general election on a still further extended franchise was approaching. The lesson of 1868–70 had evidently been learnt. On May 17, 1885, Manning wrote to Sir Charles Dilke: ' The General Election is not far off and I am very anxious to talk with you upon the point which will determine the Catholic vote.' Three weeks later Gladstone's government resigned, and preparations for the election began.

But Manning was not alone in taking action against the 1870 Act. The Radical movement for gratuitous education, which had died down after the Liberal defeat of 1874, was revived by Joseph Chamberlain in the closing years of the second Gladstone administration. A general election was due in November 1885, and in the summer and autumn of that year Chamberlain undertook a highly successful electioneering tour in support of what he called ' free schools,' which was widely taken to mean the abolition of school fees in the board schools only. Voluntary schools would either have to follow

H

suit, which they could ill afford, accept rate aid and come under the authority of the boards, or be closed. *The Radical Programme*, published in July with a preface by Chamberlain, referred without equivocation to the possible closing of voluntary schools. In October, indeed, Chamberlain made it clear that he favoured making education gratuitous in all elementary schools, whether board or voluntary, by means of an increased grant-in-aid, but he added that 'secular instruction' in voluntary schools receiving aid should be under 'popular representative control,' that is under the school-boards.

This was a proposal that Manning was unwilling to accept. 'The B. [Birmingham] scheme is " Give us your children, they shall cost you nothing; and we will stamp them with our trade-mark," ' he wrote to Bishop Vaughan on October 23, and in the same month published an article in all the Catholic newspapers, entitled 'How shall Catholics vote at the coming Parliamentary Election?' Catholics were advised to put two questions to their local candidates: (i) ' Will you do your utmost to place voluntary schools on an equal footing with board-schools?' (ii) ' Will you do your utmost to obtain a Royal Commission to review the present state of education in England and Wales, and especially the act of 1870 and its administration by the Schools Boards?' ' As they answer Yes or No, let us decide,' concluded the Cardinal.

There seems to have been no precedent for such archiepiscopal intervention in a general election, which must have required considerable courage, a fact appreciated by that hammer of the Liberals, George Denison (the Archdeacon of Taunton and many years previously one of Newman's fellow-members of the Oriel Senior Common-Room), who now wrote from East Brent (December 13, 1885) to express ' humble thankfulness to God ' for Manning's efforts and to contrast them with ' the grievous shortcomings of *our* Episcopate, our Clergy, our People in the matter of the dealing by the Civil Power with the primary question of the Religious character of the course of daily teaching permitted in the schools of England.'

The effectiveness of Manning's action is rather harder to assess, particularly in view of the fact that just before the beginning of polling Parnell published his famous manifesto to the Irish electors of Great Britain urging them to vote against all Liberal and Radical candidates—advice whose effect in many constituencies was the same as that of Manning's questionnaire. Together Parnell and the Cardinal played their part, together with other factors, in depriving the Liberal Party of the majority in the House of Commons it had enjoyed since 1880. With characteristic frankness Chamberlain acknowledged the check administered by 'the five Ps—priests, publicans, parsons, Parnellites and protectionists.' The remark was not polite, but neither was it inaccurate.

Manning's own estimate of the situation was expressed in a letter written to Vaughan a month after the election (December 20, 1885):

What strikes me is this.

1. The Parliament of 1869 [sic] gave to the Liberals and the Nonconformists a complete supremacy. The Act of 1870 was founded upon the Secular and Nonconformist basis. It has established and endowed the Nonconformist education.

2. The Parliament and Government of 1885 is the first reaction against 1870, and the Christian schools have a chance.

3. The Act of 1870 will not be repealed: and the Board-Schools cannot be broken up.

4. But an Act may be framed which will check the profuse expenditure, and multiplication of Board-Schools, and restore to Christian Schools their freedom of multiplication.

5. What more can be done? If we were asked what should we say?

6. What we need is a *permanent* settlement and protection against Chamberlain and Jules Ferry.

Already however the Hawarden kite had been flown. Soon the new Gladstonian-Parnellite alliance was to out-vote the Salisbury administration and push aside all political questions save that of Irish home rule. But one of Salisbury's last actions as Prime Minister was to set up a royal commission to study the working of the education acts. Manning was appointed a member. The second of his electoral aims had been achieved.

Two years later the commission returned majority and minority reports. The majority report, signed by Manning, recommended that the voluntary schools should be assisted out of the rates.

It was a recommendation that betokened considerable optimism—an optimism that was not consonant with an understanding of political realities. No Prime Minister who remembered the trouble caused to the first Gladstone administration by the agitation against Clause 25 of the 1870 Act could be expected to sponsor such a proposal, which would in fact have directly threatened the new Unionist alliance. Lord Salisbury declined to put 'Rome on the rates,' thereby displaying a keener appreciation of what was electorally possible than did his less cautious nephew fourteen years later.

The Catholic Marquess of Ripon (one of the comparatively few Liberal peers who had remained with Gladstone in 1886) was equally circumspect. From his seat at Studley Royal he wrote (November 18, 1888):

I am afraid that I have the misfortune of differing very materially from your Eminence upon the subject of educational policy. I stated my views to you when I saw you and the Bishop of Salford at your House. I am convinced that the wise course for Catholics to pursue is to hold firmly to what they have got and not to risk that by seeking after more.

It seems to me highly improbable in the present state of political affairs that the Government will attempt to carry out the contested proposals of the Royal Commission, but if they were to do so and to succeed in passing a Bill for that purpose through Parliament they would raise up a storm which in a few years would sweep away not only the new arrangements; but most of, if not all, the advantages which our Schools now possess. I look forward, I must honestly say, to any such attempt with the greatest alarm.

I have carefully abstained out of respect for your Eminence from expressing my opinions in public upon this subject, though I have often doubted whether, looking to the threatening aspect of affairs, I ought not to raise a warning voice before it is too late.

I only hope that I may be mistaken, but I have some experience of public affairs, and everything which has passed since the Report of the Royal Commission was published has strengthened me in the opinion which, as your Eminence knows, I have always steadily maintained.

There are administrative improvements in favour of our Schools which can and ought to be made. Legislative changes, especially such as are proposed by the Commission, will be fraught with the gravest danger.

Despite such discouragement, Manning persisted in his efforts to secure the adoption of the majority report. He published another pamphlet, *Fifty Reasons why the Voluntary Schools ought to share in the Rates,* copies of which appear to have been sent to all the members of Lord Salisbury's cabinet. Manning received polite but vague letters of acknowledgement from most, if not all of them, expressing thanks, interest and a resolve to read the work. The question of the schools appeared to have been shelved.

Then, in 1891, a few months before the dissolution of Parliament, Lord Salisbury's government introduced and carried a bill which, by according all aided schools a new grant of ten shillings per child in average attendance to replace the fees, in effect made education gratuitous in all primary schools, whether board or voluntary.

It does not appear that Manning, now eighty-three years of age, took any part in the negotiations that preceded the passing of this act. In any case the terms of the act were not in accordance with the ideas that he had put forward in the majority report of the commission and in his numerous pamphlets and articles. The 1891 act did not touch the dangerous question of rate-aid to voluntary schools; it did make education gratuitous. Manning had been pressing for rate-aid for twenty years; on the other hand he did not believe in gratuitous education—on the contrary, the majority report specifically declared itself in favour of the continued payment by parents of school fees.

Thus the act of 1891, while it conferred important financial benefits on Catholic schools, did not constitute the settlement that Manning himself would have preferred. It is probable, indeed, that the consideration that led to the passing of the act was not so much a belief in the desirability of what is popularly known as ' free education,' as the realization that a Liberal majority in the next House of Commons might well render board-school education gratuitous, without voting any commensurate grant to the voluntary schools. Such a policy had been hinted at in *The Radical Programme* in 1885, and the minority report of the education commission had contained the ominous statement that ' no practicable scheme for universal free schools, consistent with the continuance of the voluntary school system, has been presented to us.' To Salisbury and his colleagues, faced with the possibility of electoral defeat and an ensuing threat to the very existence of the voluntary schools, the abrogation of parental responsibility which the new act involved may well have appeared as a comparatively minor evil.

Thus it was not until 1902 that the aim towards which Manning had striven was achieved, and the disturbances that followed the passing of the Balfour act may well be regarded as a justification of the caution displayed during Manning's lifetime by the practical Conservative politicians of the day. Manning failed in fact to achieve the legislative equality that he had sought, and though he may perhaps have welcomed the financial benefits that in the closing months of his own life the new education act brought to the Catholic schools, he can hardly have rejoiced at the moral principle which that act embodied. Indeed it is upon his resistance to the Radical proposals of the eighties, rather than upon any positive legislative achievement in his own life-time, that Manning's claim to a place in educational history must be said to rest.

VIII

MANNING AND IRELAND

By Denis Gwynn

MANNING's intense awareness of the Irish preponderance among the Catholics in England during his lifetime appears very clearly in his biographies. In December 1882, looking back upon the fifty years since he preached his first sermon as an Anglican curate, and comparing his own record with Gladstone's 'political jubilee' at the same time, he recorded[1] in his diary: 'I remember saying that I had "given up working for the people of England to work for the Irish occupation in England." But that occupation is a part of the Church throughout the world, of an empire greater than the British.' The same phrase recurs frequently in his later years. In February 1887, contrasting himself with another, he writes again: 'His whole life was spent in working for the English people. So I began in a little, and then have spent my life in working for the Irish occupation in England. But that occupation is the Catholic Church in all the amplitude of faith, grace, and authority.'

The main impact of the Irish immigration, during the desolating famine of 1845-47 and the years that followed it, had taken effect before Manning became a Catholic in 1851, at the age of forty-three. He had scarcely any direct experience of the Irish immigrants while he lived in Sussex, either at the village rectory of Lavington or at Chichester where he had become Archdeacon. But when he came to London to work with Cardinal Wiseman in the early fifties the problems that had been caused by the vast influx of poor Irish Catholics were present on all sides. And when, as Provost of Westminster, he succeeded Wiseman as Archbishop in 1865 he was deeply preoccupied both with the Irish Catholics in England and with the wider questions which caused their estrangement from English life. That estrangement persisted

---

[1] Purcell, II, p. 677.

until after his death, but he had laboured incessantly to overcome it.   At the very end of his life, when he composed his
celebrated memorandum on the ' Hindrances to the Spread
of Catholicism in England,' he stressed again the preponderance of the Irish Catholics and the difficulty of reconciling
them to the social and political conditions of the country.   He
reckoned that, out of some 1,200,000 Catholics then in England,
a million were Irish.

> The 200,000 English Catholics [he wrote] have much of
> John Bull in them, but the million of our people are born
> into an animosity against Queen Elizabeth, Cromwell, and
> William III.   It is with difficulty that our people will
> petition Parliament for anything.   Once it was my fate to
> ask the people at St Mary's to sign a Petition to Parliament.
> The Petition lay for signature in the school next to my house.
> I found that a young Irishman had emptied the ink-bottle
> over it as a protest against Parliament!
> By the law of nature a people grows up into social and
> civil life on the soil where they are born.   By the sin and
> persecution of England this has never been true of the people
> of Ireland.   They are the most Christian people on the face
> of the earth.   But not the most civilized in Gioberti's sense.
> Christianity is their civilization, and before God it is the
> highest, but for this world it is not so.   We have a million
> of people, priests, and faithful of Irish blood, faith and
> civilization in England, and they are not only alienated from
> our laws and legislature, but would upset the ink-bottle over
> the Statute book. . . .   A capacity for civil and public
> action needs, of course, a training and education, but it
> springs from a love of our country.   The Irish have this
> intensely for Ireland, but can hardly have it as yet for
> England.

For thirty years he had been in high authority at Westminster, either as Provost or as Archbishop, when he wrote
those last reflections in 1890; and there had been a lessening
of the earlier tension during that time.   The bitter memories
of the famine and of the enforced exodus were already growing
remote, to the generation of Irish Catholics that knew him as
the Cardinal Archbishop who had made himself their champion and protector in England.   But his first years as Archbishop had included the Fenian agitation, both in Ireland

and in England; and he had identified himself directly then
with a bold programme of radical reforms in Ireland. In
June 1865 he was consecrated Archbishop of Westminster;
and it was within the few following years that both Gladstone
and Disraeli became the official leaders of their parties. The
outbreak of Fenian activity in 1867 compelled both to devote
close attention to Irish discontent; and Manning as the new
Archbishop of Westminster gave his advice forcibly to both.
He had known Gladstone intimately since they were at Oxford
together; and there had been a time when Wiseman and his
friends had hoped, after the Gorham Judgment, that Gladstone
would become a Catholic at the same time as Manning and
their friend the barrister, James Hope, Q.C.

Cardinal Cullen had been Archbishop of Dublin since 1851,
and had used all his great influence to discourage the restless
tendencies of Irish nationalism. Manning's radical politics
were out of sympathy with Cullen's intense conservatism;
but Manning realized how completely Cullen dominated the
Irish bishops, and as Wiseman's successor, he set himself to
establish close relations between the Irish and the English
hierarchies. He found that Cullen was concerned chiefly
to obtain two reforms: the provision of Catholic education
at all stages, and the disestablishment of the Protestant Church
in Ireland. Manning prepared to give his utmost support
on both issues; but his first years as Archbishop coincided with
the Fenian disorders which aroused anti-Irish feeling in England. The Irish bishops followed Cullen in denouncing
Fenianism on all sides, and Manning issued similar denuncia-
tions in England. He welcomed the opportunity of showing
that the Church was always on the side of public order, and
he wrote to Cullen that he had ' never known a more propi-
tious moment to make the Government feel that they cannot
do without us.'

But the overwhelming evidence of Irish sympathy in England
with Fenianism convinced Manning that the time had come
for a vigorous attempt to remove the causes of Irish discontent.
While he denounced secret societies and revolutionary principles, he was deeply moved by the religious sincerity of the
Fenian prisoners who asked that Mass should be said for them
in jails, and he succeeded in obtaining their request. ' My

heart bleeds for those who are deceived by their higher and nobler affections,' he wrote in his diary. ' They believe themselves to be serving in a sacred and holy war for their country and religion.' His Lenten pastoral of 1867 dealt with Fenianism, and he sent copies of it to both Gladstone and Disraeli, writing[1] in a letter which accompanied the pastoral, ' I cannot overstate my anxiety on this subject. Nothing will lessen it but a large and adequate policy for Ireland.'

Lord Derby was still Prime Minister in 1867, of a Ministry which could not last much longer because the House of Commons had no reliable party majority; and Lord Russell was still leader of the Liberal Party. But within the following year both Derby and Russell had retired, and Disraeli and Gladstone were the new party leaders. There was no apparent hope that either party would pay heed to Cardinal Cullen's demand for disestablishment of the Irish Church; but Disraeli was prepared to give a charter to a Catholic University in Ireland, though without any endowment. Manning acted as intermediary in London, and gave Cullen his own opinion that the charter should be accepted, but found that the Irish bishops would oppose any Bill which did not provide for endowment. In December 1867, Lord Russell announced that he would retire from the party leadership in favour of Gladstone; and in the following February Disraeli succeeded Lord Derby as Prime Minister. Manning had by that time informed Disraeli that Cardinal Cullen was willing to accept the Catholic University without endowment; and when it was subsequently repudiated by the Irish bishops, Disraeli accused Manning of having ' stabbed him in the back.' Manning found that he could not explain the position without declaring that he disagreed with the Irish bishops, and relations between him and the new Prime Minister were broken for a time.

But Manning had already decided to put forward his personal programme of Irish reforms on a much wider scale; and in March 1868 he published a pamphlet entitled *Ireland: A Letter to Earl Grey*, which provides a vivid statement of the policies which represented his whole attitude towards Ireland in all the following years. Disraeli had become Prime Minister

---

[1] Leslie, p. 177.

in the month before the pamphlet was published, and Gladstone had been leader of the Liberal party since December. It
was evident that Disraeli's Ministry could not continue for
long without a new general election; and Manning was
engaged in consultations with both leaders concerning the
proposed Catholic University. He reported to Cardinal Cullen
on March 14 that after an interview with Disraeli he 'felt
no doubt that he sincerely intends to carry his proposal' if
the Irish bishops would accept it. He was convinced also that
Gladstone would not oppose it. The adverse decision by the
Irish bishops produced a rupture between Manning and
Disraeli. But he had already sent to both Disraeli and Gladstone copies of his pamphlet on Ireland, which was dated
March 12, 1868. It called for an immediate disestablishment
of the Protestant Church in Ireland and a total repeal of all
anti-Catholic laws on the Statute book.

In a private letter[1] to Gladstone which accompanied the
pamphlet on March 11, Manning wrote:

It gives expression to feelings and convictions which
powerfully govern the great mass of our people, who desire
to see Great Britain and Ireland strong and peaceful.
Believe me, the only hope of restoring Ireland to social
order and peace is to give free course to the only powers
of Christianity which control it. Weaken these in the
upper classes, as they have been by various causes weakened
in the lower, and you will have to deal with '98 over again.
A true, full, unimpeded Catholic education is the only hope
I know of keeping Ireland from American anarchy. For I
know you do not wish either for the Duke of Cumberland
with 24,000 men or with *The Times* for an Indian mutiny
or a Jamaica massacre.

He could hope for nothing from Disraeli at this stage, though
their consultations over the proposed Catholic University
had not yet broken down. But from Gladstone it was just
possible to obtain a hearing for the demand for Church
Disestablishment. They had discussed it often in the past;
and Manning had urged it upon him more than twenty years
before, in 1845, when even Newman had not yet become a
Catholic and when Manning was still unshaken in his Anglican

---

[1] Leslie, p. 205.

convictions. 'You may go on calling it the Irish Church and the Established Church, but it is a mere phrase,' Manning had written to Gladstone in 1845. 'The work of the sixteenth century is undone in Ireland. It is a question of first principles.' Gladstone himself had pondered over the question in the interval, and he, too, had been convinced that the Irish Church must sooner or later be disestablished. But he had voted against a motion for its disestablishment in 1865, on the ground that the time had not yet come; and again in 1866 he had supported Lord Russell in opposing another motion for it.

But disestablishment of the Church of Ireland was only one of the bold proposals which Manning set forth in the letter to Earl Grey which appeared as a pamphlet in March 1868. It was addressed to Earl Grey, he explained, 'because your Lordship has long stood aloof from the two great parties in the state: and in what I write I desire to hold myself neutral between opposing sides. I make an appeal for justice, not to one side or the other, but to both.' As an Englishman whose 'national bias was on the side of England,' he could ' at least claim to be impartial.' But his special acquaintance with Irish people in England during many years convinced him that the ' gravity of the present crisis could not be overrated.' He believed it to be ' of a graver, deeper, mightier, and more permanent character than the risings of 1798 or of 1803.' He stressed the 'international organizations which unite Ireland to the continent of Europe, and the intimate and vital bond which links Ireland to America.' These developments were, he believed, ' gradually assimilating and changing an integral part of the United Kingdom into a type which will hardly combine with ours, or consolidate the unity of these realms.'

Two questions, he said, demanded immediate remedy, ' but the power of controlling them is becoming less and less as they are continually postponed.' They could ' all be summed up in two general heads, Religious Equality and an equitable Land-Law.' But beyond these practical issues lay the wider problem that English rule in Ireland was thought to be ' wrong, tyrannical and unjust.' ' To our own hurt,' he asserted, ' we have made the English name hateful in the past, and we must bear the penalty till we have repaired the wrong.' The root cause of Fenianism was animosity against England, and he asked, ' Has that animosity nothing to do with the three confiscations of almost every acre of land in Ireland, and the folly of striving for three hundred years to force the Reformation on a Catholic people? ' The Fenian agitation was a direct sequel to the early revolutionary movements of 1798, 1828 and 1848, which had been powerfully influenced by revolutionary movements on the Continent. But this time, in 1868, ' not the Continent only, but America is in direct and hostile action upon all the elements of disorder, and, what is more dangerous, upon all the causes of just discontent in this country.'

Enumerating the ' causes of just discontent in Ireland ' which the Legislature had not yet attempted to remove, Manning declared:

> So long as there exists upon the Statute-book any penal enactment against the Catholic religion; so long as the Catholic people of Ireland are deprived of a *bona fide* Catholic education; so long as a Protestant Church Establishment is maintained by law over the face of Catholic Ireland, and so long as the people of Ireland fail to derive from the land such a subsistence as the labourers and farmers of England and Scotland derive from the soil: there must be a just discontent, which will be the misery of Ireland and the danger of England.

The remedies which he urged were radical; but in several directions they could be applied immediately. The first was to be ' an Act of Parliament summed up in one clause which would recite and repeal all penal enactments against the Catholic Church and religion still lingering in the Statutes of these realms.' If Ireland was to be ' justly pacified, the Church of the people must be placed upon the perfect equality which it enjoys in Canada and Australia.' His second remedy, ' which could be passed at once if any Government have the will to do so,' was to produce ' such a modification of the National Education Board as shall make the existing schools *bona fide* denominational schools of the Catholic and of the Protestant populations respectively.' The existing system was ' distasteful to Catholics and to Protestants alike.' He showed that in 2,454 of the schools in Ireland, with 374,000 Catholic children, there was not one Protestant child; and in 2,483 others there were only 24,000 Protestant children but 321,640 Catholic children. Thus, in nearly 5,000 of the Irish national schools there were some 25,000 Protestant children and 700,000 Catholics; yet the Catholic children in them could not be taught the Catholic religion, nor use Catholic books, nor even put up a crucifix. Although in England the national system was Anglican, and in Scotland, Presbyterian, in the Irish schools the Catholic religion was prohibited, ' in deference to a small number of Protestants.' On what principle of common justice, he asked, could a Catholic denominational education be refused to the Catholic people in Ireland?

From these more general demands, Manning passed boldly to a demand for Disestablishment of the Protestant Church in Ireland.

England tried for a century to force Episcopacy upon Scotland. It has tried for three to force Protestantism upon Ireland. England had the timely wisdom to leave Scotland to its own religion. Let it have the tardy wisdom to leave Ireland to its faith. It may as well try to change the saltness of the sea as to make the Irish people Protestants. They have multiplied from the remnant of Connaught to a people which outnumbers fourfold their Protestant brethren, and overspreads in its dispersion the colonies of Great Britain and the United States of America. The dream of conversion is long since dispelled for ever. There does not remain a shadow of reason or of justice for the hostile Church which for three hundred years has overspread the whole Catholic people of Ireland. Nay, more than this, it has become a danger to the Empire, and a reproach to England in the eyes of the whole Christian and civilized world.

He emphasized the recent declaration by the Irish Catholic bishops that they would never accept any endowment of their own Church from the funds which were now devoted to the Protestant Church, but that they urged that the funds should be used for the benefit of the poor.

The question of applying the proceeds [Manning wrote] be it easy or difficult of solution, in no way bears upon the absolute duty of withdrawing from Catholic Ireland the ubiquitous offence and challenge of a Protestant Establishment in every diocese and in every parish, where sometimes the whole population is exclusively Catholic. Perfect religious equality, as in Canada and Australia, is the sole way of peace and justice between England and Ireland.

On these questions of religious toleration and equality, Manning's title to speak was incontestable. But he embarked deliberately on the more controversial question of Irish land tenure, with an assertion of social principles which bears a close analogy to the doctrines which he expounded in his lecture at Leeds on the Dignity and Rights of Labour in the following year. The Irish Land question, he declared, ' is the chief and paramount condition on which the peace of Ireland depends. In comparison with this question, all others are light. It is the question of the people and of the poor, of social peace or agrarian war; of life or of death, to millions.' He denied that it involved any special complexity, and he set forth ' some general truths and governing axioms connected with it, about which there can be no reasonable doubt.'

I will begin, then, by affirming that there is a natural and divine law, anterior and superior to all human and civil law, by which every people has a right to live of the fruits of the soil on which they are born, and in which they are buried. This is a right older and higher than any personal right. It is the intrinsic right of the whole people and society, out of which all private rights to the soil and its fruits are created, and by which those created rights must always be controlled. A starving man commits no theft if he saves his life by eating of his neighbour's bread so much as is necessary for the support of his existence. The civil law yields before the higher jurisdiction of the divine, as the positive divine law yields before the natural law of God.

This simple doctrine had in fact been treated as a blasphemy against ' law and order ' during the famine years in Ireland, when the Irish land system had produced precisely the conditions that Manning now described. He had come to realize that Fenianism was the direct outcome of that injustice and its terrible consequences at that time. He presented the case now in plain terms which, in Ireland, would have been denounced and punished by law as direct incitement to agrarian revolt. Though he lived in London, he could speak with intimate knowledge of rural conditions in southern England: and only a few years later he was to give invaluable assistance to Joseph Arch as the founder of the Agricultural Workers' Union.

English tenants are protected by the mightiest power that ever ruled a Christian country—a power which controls the Legislature, dictates the Laws, and guides even the sovereignty of the Crown—the force of a vigilant, watchful, ubiquitous public opinion. But in Ireland none of these things are so. In one-fourth of Ireland, there are land laws, or, rather, land customs, which protect the tenant. In three-fourths of Ireland, there are neither laws nor customs. The tenants are tenants at will. Over a vast proportion of Ireland, the landlords are absentees. The mitigating and restraining influences of the lords of the soil which, in England, and in every civilized country, do more to correct the excesses of agents, speculators, and traffickers, and to temper legal rights with equity and moderation, are hardly to be found. The substantial improvements upon farms, and the buildings necessary for agriculture, are made, not by the landlord, as in England, but by the tenant in Ireland. Is this to be found in any other country of Europe? The tenant has no security that his outlay is his own, or that he shall ever reap the benefit of it. . . . The landlord may raise his rent at will, and give him notice to quit at will. The tenant at will may be put out for any cause; not only for non-payment of rent, or waste of his land, or bad farming, or breach of covenant, if such can be supposed to exist, all of which would bear a colour of justice; but for the personal advantage of the landlord arising from the tenant's improvements; for political influence; for caprice, for any passing reason or no reason, assigned, or not assignable, which can arise in minds conscious of absolute and irresponsible power. . . .

If the evils which have passed in Ireland since 1810 had passed in England, the public opinion of this country would have imperiously compelled the Legislature to turn our land customs into Acts of Parliament. If any sensible proportion of the people of the English counties were to be seen moving down upon the Thames for embarkation to America, and dropping by the roadside from hunger and fever, and it had been heard by the wayside that they were ' tenants at will,' evicted for any cause whatsoever, the public opinion of the country would have arisen to render impossible the repetition of such absolute and irresponsible exercise of legal rights. It would erect tribunals to judge between landlords and tenants; it would reduce to open and legal process the exercise of these imperial rights claimed by private citizens. If five millions, that is, a fourth of the English people, had either emigrated in a mass, by reason of discontent, misery, or eviction, or had died by fever and by famine since the year 1848, the whole land system of England would have been modified so as to render the return of such a national danger impossible for ever. But both these suppositions have been verified in Ireland.

Whole counties have been sensibly drained of their population; the public ways have been choked by departing trains of emigrants; one fourth of the population of Ireland fled from it, or died of hunger and fever, and yet the Legislature still maintain the land laws under which these things are possible. Parliament did, indeed, fifteen years ago, solemnly recognize the right of tenants, but that recognition lies dead on the record. This, too, adds bitterness to those who suffer. Their right has been acknowledged but its protection has for fifteen years been delayed.

In support of these statements, Manning gave definite instances of wholesale evictions and other forms of injustice. He believed that these evils were ' unknown to the English people at large ' and that they ' would not rest a day without crying out to be delivered from the shame of partaking, even by silence, in such atrocities.' Disclaiming any intention to propose a detailed scheme, he was asserting ' the principles which ought to govern this question.' He recalled that in 1852, Lord Derby's Ministry had introduced a Bill ' affirming the great principle of equity " That the property created by the industry of the tenant belongs of right and in justice to himself, and that it is the duty of the Legislature to protect it by law." ' That Bill had been adopted in 1853 by Lord Aberdeen's Ministry and ' supported by all the three great political parties in the State.' It had been passed by large majorities, but never became law. Manning urged its adoption now, ' from the profound conviction that the deepest and

I

sorest cause of the discontent and unrest of Ireland is the land question.' He was pleading in this sense ten years before Michael Davitt had yet founded the Irish Land League; and in the later years he could claim that his sympathy with the land agitation had been expressed long before. It had arisen from his intimate knowledge of the Irish Catholic immigrants in the English cities, and of the sufferings which compelled them to emigrate.

I am day by day in contact [he wrote in this Letter to Lord Grey] with an impoverished race driven from home by the land question. I see it daily in the destitution of my flock. The religious inequality does indeed keenly wound and excite the Irish people. Peace and good will can never reign in Ireland until every stigma is effaced from the Catholic Church and faith, and the galling injustice of religious inequality shall have been redressed. This, indeed, is true. But the ' Land Question,' as we call it, by a somewhat heartless euphemism, means hunger, thirst, nakedness, notice to quit, labour spent in vain, the toil of years seized upon, the breaking up of homes, the miseries, sicknesses, deaths, of parents, children, wives; the despair and wildness which spring up in the hearts of the poor when legal force, like a sharp harrow, goes over the most sensitive and vital rights of mankind. All this is contained in the land question. It is this intolerable grief which has driven hundreds of thousands to America, there to bide the time of return. No greater self-deception could we practise on ourselves than to imagine that Fenianism is the folly of a few apprentices and shop-boys. Fenianism could not have survived for a year if it were not sustained by the traditional and just discontent of almost a whole people.

His contacts with the Irish immigrants had given him what few others yet shared, a perception of the growing importance of the distant colonies. He was aware of the constant flow of funds from Irish emigrants in America to assist their relatives and to enable others to go there. The Irish in America alone were already more numerous than those who remained in Ireland: and ' four million and a half of Irish in Ireland turn instinctively to five million of Irish in America.' He appealed for ' a policy of absolute equality in religion ' as being indispensable 'if the empire is to hold together.' Canada and

Australia had led the way and were 'teaching the mother country how to live.' He appealed as an entirely patriotic Englishman, ' as one who, next after that which is not of this world, desires earnestly to see maintained the unity, solidity and prosperity of the British Empire.' If they would ' raise Ireland to an absolute equality, social, political and religious, with England and Scotland,' he believed they would ' win back the love and fidelity of the noble-hearted, generous, heroic people of Catholic Ireland.'

There is no evidence that Manning had even informed Gladstone that his pamphlet was in preparation, and Gladstone's swift reaction to it was startling. The pamphlet was published by Longmans at a shilling and it is signed and dated for March 12. Manning's letter to Gladstone which enclosed a copy is dated March 11. Within the following week, on March 16, Gladstone made his first public declaration in the House of Commons that ' the time had come when the Church of Ireland as a Church in alliance with the State must cease to exist.' The occasion of his pronouncement was a motion by one of the Irish members, J. F. Maguire, who called attention to the state of unrest in Ireland and attributed it, as Manning had done, to the land question and to the existence of the Established Church. Gladstone seized his opportunity of declaring a new Irish policy in his capacity as leader of the Liberal party; and in Morley's words[1] his statement ' was not a mere sounding sentence in a speech: it was one of the heroic acts of his life.' Many members of his party regarded him unfavourably as their new leader, and ' to attack the Irish Church was to alarm and scandalize his own chosen friends and closest allies in the kindred Church of England. To attack a high Protestant institution " exalting its mitred front " in the Catholic island, was to run sharp risk of awaking the sleuth-hounds of No-Popery.' But Gladstone had seized instinctively upon an issue which was likely to appeal to the new electorate. Within the following week he gave notice of three resolutions to declare that the Irish Church must be disestablished, and to make the necessary arrangements.

Manning's negotiations with Disraeli over the proposed Catholic University Charter were still in progress, and Gladstone's

---

[1] Morley's *Gladstone*, II, p. 244.

sudden advocacy of Disestablishment had, as Manning wrote to Cardinal Cullen, made it difficult to approach the Tory leader. But he had written earnest encouragements to Gladstone. ' The Irish establishment is a great wrong,' Manning wrote[1] to him when the resolutions had been notified. ' It is the cause of division in Ireland, of alienation between Ireland and England. It embitters every other question. Even the land question is exasperated by it. The fatal ascendancy of race over race is unspeakably aggravated by the ascendancy of religion over religion.' By May he was reporting[2] to Cullen that ' great progress had been made ' but that there would be a hard fight. The battle raged through the summer, but Gladstone carried his first resolution in April by a majority of 61. Disraeli advised the Queen to dissolve Parliament at once, but was willing to continue in office till the autumn when the new electoral register would be effective. In November the elections were held, and Gladstone was returned as Prime Minister for the first time, with a Liberal majority of 112, much larger than any Ministry had had for years past.

Manning's personal influence was unquestionably one of the chief causes of the Irish reforms which Gladstone introduced or attempted in his first term of office. But their relations became necessarily more distant. In congratulating him in December 1868, Manning wrote[3]: ' I fully recognize the prudence of our not meeting now. All is changed since I wrote. Had you then been what you are, I should not have written. And so you are at the end men live for, but not, I believe, the end for which you have lived. It is strange so to salute you, but very pleasant. I take much consolation from the fact that what has made you so is a cause in which my whole heart can go with you.' Gladstone spent all Christmas in drafting the lines of his Irish Church Bill. In March it was introduced in the Commons, and by June opposition had been so strongly organized that a collision between the Commons and the House of Lords seemed inevitable. But Gladstone's firmness overbore the fears of the Queen and compelled the Lords to accept terms, and before August the Bill had passed all its stages. Manning had been advising Gladstone steadily on many

---

[1] Morley, II, p. 246.   [2] Leslie, p. 198.   [3] *Ibid.*, p. 201.

difficult questions; especially concerning the old endowments, which Cardinal Cullen wisely desired to disregard, though some of the leading laymen wished to claim them in part for Catholic purposes. When the Bill was finally passed in July, Gladstone wrote to Manning a letter thanking him for his ' firm, constant and discriminating support during the arduous conflict.'

It was the most important concession won for Ireland since the Emancipation Act of forty years earlier; and Manning had not only assisted it powerfully, but was responsible for Gladstone's sudden decision to attempt it. His pamphlet on Ireland had largely provided the programme of Gladstone's first Ministry; and after disestablishing the Irish Church in 1869 Gladstone proceeded to apply Manning's principles to the Irish Land problem. He had appointed as Irish Secretary Mr. Chichester Fortescue, who had previously introduced a private Bill to establish the principle that tenants should be entitled to their own improvements. But scarcely any other member of his Cabinet except John Bright had any knowledge of Irish conditions. Gladstone devoted months to mastering the question before confronting the Cabinet with the Bill to which he won their consent. Manning urged him to adopt bolder and more practical measures, to introduce a system of fixing judicial rents and a guarantee of tenure; but at this stage Gladstone would not attempt more than to curtail the land-lord's power of eviction, while asserting the principle that compensation must be given for improvements. After intro-ducing his Bill Gladstone wrote[1] to Manning privately to claim that it would at least ' prevent the landlord from using the terrible weapon of undue and unjust eviction, by so framing the handle that it shall cut his hands with the sharp edge of pecuniary damages. The man evicted without any fault, and suffering the usual loss by it, will receive whatever the custom of the country gives, and where there is no custom, according to a scale, besides whatever he can claim for permanent buildings or reclamation of land. Wanton eviction will, as I hope, be extinguished by provisions like these.'

As a measure of land reform, it was utterly inadequate, but it did at least introduce for the first time the principle that the

---

[1] Morley, II, p. 284.

Irish tenant had some right in the land he occupied. While
Gladstone was astonishing his friends by carrying the Bill
almost without opposition through both Houses, Manning
had to convey to him formal messages from the Irish bishops,
who demanded land courts to revise rents and a legal recognition that tenants could not be evicted if they paid. Nevertheless, the Irish Land Act of 1870 became the foundation of all
subsequent progress. As Lecky wrote afterwards, it compelled
every Ministry from that time onward ' to base all their
legislation on the doctrine that Irish land is not an undivided
ownership, but a simple partnership.' At Manning's instiga-
tion, Gladstone had within two years established that legal
principle, even without opposition in the House of Lords,
besides carrying the Disestablishment of the Irish Church.
In the same Ministry, he attempted also to deal with education;
and his attempt to settle the vexed question of Irish University
education led to his downfall. Once again he was in consulta-
tion with Manning, and Manning's awareness of the political
difficulties in England made him willing to accept proposals
which the Irish bishops would not consider. He had urged
Cardinal Cullen in 1869 to accept Disraeli's offer of a Catholic
University without endowment; and Gladstone now offered
in 1873 a new measure, with certain endowments. But it
was not to be a Catholic University. There were to be no
religious tests, and Gladstone's Bill excluded from the university, though not from its separate colleges, all teaching of
theology or modern history or moral and mental philosophy.
Manning was so far satisfied with these proposals that he wrote
to Cullen strongly urging acceptance; and when the Irish
bishops refused, he advised Gladstone against undue discouragement. But Cardinal Cullen's open denunciation of
the Bill as an attempt to consolidate and extend the ' godless '
Queen's Colleges made acceptance in Ireland impossible.
Cullen's opposition caused a reaction among Gladstone's supporters in England, and in March he was defeated on an amendment to the Bill, and he offered his resignation to the Queen.
    In January 1874 another general election brought back
Disraeli as Prime Minister, and Gladstone retired for a time
from leadership of his party. Manning's influence in politics
declined immediately; but he had been alarmed by the growing

dependence of Gladstone on the Nonconformists, and was content to wait for later opportunities. He had become converted to the principle of Home Rule while Cullen was still opposed to it, but it was Cullen who had sent him Isaac Butt's masterly work on *Land Tenure in Ireland* which had provided the most effective evidence in his pamphlet letter to Earl Grey. Butt was a Protestant lawyer in Dublin who had been professor of political economy. In his earlier years he was the ablest defender of the Act of Union, but he lost all faith in the capacity of the British Parliament to legislate for Ireland, during the famine. In his old age he had formed the Irish Home Rule Association and become leader of a new Nationalist party at Westminster. Manning had been convinced by Butt's advocacy of Home Rule before he published his pamphlet on Ireland in 1868, but he kept his views to himself until Irish affairs became an urgent problem again with the acute distress of 1879, which resulted in Michael Davitt's founding the Land League. Davitt himself had been a Fenian while he worked in a mill in Lancashire, and he had been imprisoned as a convict in England during the years when the Fenian prisoners had been a constant reminder of Irish discontent.

While Disraeli was Prime Minister, since the beginning of 1874, Gladstone was no longer in the House of Commons; but the ' Midlothian campaign ' at the end of 1879 brought him suddenly out of his retirement. It coincided with the revival of intense agrarian troubles in Ireland, and in the early months of 1880 Disraeli hoped confidently for a successful election by denouncing Irish agitation and especially its younger exponents, Parnell and Biggar, in the House of Commons. But Gladstone's vehement return to public life swept the country, and the new House of Commons had nearly 350 Liberals against 240 Conservatives, with 65 Irish Nationalists, of whom more than half were followers of Parnell. Manning, a year older than Gladstone, was now seventy-two; but his political views had become increasingly radical. To one of Gladstone's colleagues he wrote[1] in May after the election: ' You have been lifted upon the top of the wave which nobody looked for; and you will have to deal with Ireland, and will be better able to deal with it than others. I am very Irish in

---

[1] Leslie, p. 382.

my sympathies, and I hope for some measure which will be felt in the homes of the poor.' He sent what he described as a 'very full and strong letter' to Cardinal Simeoni about Ireland, but he felt the need to restrain his own feelings. In writing to Herbert Vaughan in Rome, he said cautiously, 'we cannot risk the mission to the English nation for the Irish. Were we to take a very radical line just now, we might identify the Church with Radicalism and revolution in the minds of the English.'

Cardinal Cullen was dead, and he had been succeeded by Archbishop McCabe in Dublin; but the most influential figure in the Irish hierarchy now was Archbishop Croke of Cashel. Croke's sympathies with the Land League and with Parnell's active leadership were expressed openly, and Manning shared them, though he frequently regretted the effects of Croke's courageous speaking. Gladstone had found it necessary to introduce a new Land Act which went much further than his Act of 1870, by providing for fair rent courts and recognizing fixity of tenure. He had taken drastic action against the Land League and imprisoned Parnell and a number of his colleagues, but the Land Bill went forward, with Manning acting as a constant intermediary between the Government and the Irish bishops. He had urged them to give the Bill their formal approval, but many of them felt that their recommendations had been 'utterly ignored by Mr. Gladstone.' McCabe wrote to him, however, that ' we all feel that in your Eminence Ireland has a very sincere friend.' He had won their confidence so fully that he could write freely to Archbishop Croke. He disapproved strongly of Parnell's defiant obstruction in the House of Commons, which ' has unspeakably damaged the cause of Ireland,' and he wrote that the ' disastrous events which have surrounded the Land League have made just men regard it with suspicion and hostility.' He hoped that Croke's hands might be ' strong to keep the Land League within the lines of right and law.'

Croke's sympathies were with Parnell, but he responded with sincere gratitude to the efforts which Manning was making to ensure land reform. He urged that a release of political prisoners was indispensable, especially of Father Sheehy who had been imprisoned on charges of inciting to riot. And he believed that Manning greatly overestimated the danger of revolutionary principles being introduced from America or from France. Manning had written to him : ' My desire is to see you and the Irish Episcopate leading and uniting the people as in old times, and all the more because we are now not dealing with Ireland in Ireland, but with America in Ireland as I fear.' Croke replied confidently, with his intimate knowledge of the people: ' There is nothing to be dreaded, I assure your Eminence, from what is called the " French Alliance," for the very valid reason that it is an alliance *in nubibus*; nor, indeed, from any other sinister influence, and I think I can safely say that the Irish people were never more reasonably religious than they are today, and as a rule so thoroughly devoted to their clergy.'

These friendly relations were to have extremely important results when Cardinal McCabe died in February 1885, and the Foreign Office attempted to influence Rome in the appointment of his successor. Sir George Errington had been already employed in Rome as a diplomatic agent, and he had the confidence both of Cardinal McCabe and of the Government. The archbishopric of Dublin was a vitally important see, and Lord Granville sent Errington to Rome to ensure that it would not be filled by a bishop who had given support to the Land League. But the Irish bishops, and particularly Croke, regarded Dr. Walsh, the President of Maynooth, as being supremely qualified for nomination; and he had received a decisive majority in the recommendations of the Dublin clergy. Dr. Walsh had shown great abilities and scholarship at Maynooth and, though he was naturally conservative, he had written vigorously in support of Irish land reforms. The newspapers had begun to forecast his succession to Dublin, and Granville instructed Errington to do his utmost in Rome to prevent it. Davitt happened to be in Rome, in an effort to enlist Papal sympathy for the Land League, and he was there after Easter when almost all the Irish bishops arrived at the same time for their *ad limina* visits. Diplomatic influences on both sides were brought into vigorous play, and it became known that Errington had asked that the Dublin see should be filled not by Dr. Walsh but by Cardinal Cullen's nephew, Dr. Moran, who had recently gone to Australia as Archbishop of

Sydney. Manning in London had special sources of information through his friendship with Sir Charles Dilke, who was under-secretary for Foreign Affairs; and Dilke was strongly opposed to such unofficial negotiations at the Vatican. Both by private information and by exerting his personal influence, Manning gave invaluable assistance on behalf of Dr. Walsh. Croke wrote from Rome to inform[1] Manning that ' the setting aside of Dr. Walsh *for anyone* would raise such a storm in Ireland and in the United States that His Holiness should be solemnly warned against doing so. Your Eminence alone can give such a warning *and I earnestly ask you to do it.*'

Manning at once wrote to Leo XIII, emphasizing not only the worthiness of Dr. Walsh and the united wish of the Irish bishops for his appointment, but also the ' supreme danger of even *seeming* to be swayed from England.' At the same time he sent a formal letter to Dilke, placing on record what he had told him privately, and authorizing him to ' use it as you see fit.' In the meantime Dr. Moran had been definitely summoned to Rome, and anxiety in Ireland grew intense. Croke reported to Manning in June, after his return to Ireland, that ' things look very threatening here. The people cannot be persuaded that the Pope has not entered into some sort of agreement with the Government, the price paid by His Holiness being the setting aside of the popular candidate for the See of Dublin and the appointment of some cold and colourless ecclesiastic.' His own conversation with the Pope had made him apprehensive that political influences might prevail, and he wrote[2] earnestly to inform Manning of his fears, ' as the highest and most influential ecclesiastic within the realm, with the hope that you may have it conveyed to the proper quarter.' Manning complied all the more readily because he was deeply impressed by Dr. Walsh's abilities and character and by his record as President of Maynooth. He was in constant contact with Dilke because they were at this time both members of the Royal Commission on the Housing of the Working Classes, and he used his opportunities fully. Dilke's diaries and letters give ample evidence of Manning's activity and of his insistence that British diplomacy should not interfere in the appointment.

---

[1] *Life of Archbishop Walsh*, p. 154.   [2] *Ibid.*, p. 156.

While the decision was still in suspense, Gladstone's Ministry was suddenly defeated by the Irish vote in June 1885, and Lord Salisbury became Prime Minister. Manning's support from Dilke was no longer available: and it seemed that the new Ministry would continue Errington's intrigues in Rome. Manning made it his business to meet the new Viceroy, Lord Carnarvon, before he left for Ireland, and impressed upon him the dangers of interference. But within a few days Leo XIII had appointed Dr. Walsh as Archbishop of Dublin, and the strain was lifted. Manning's efforts had earned him the gratitude and confidence of the Irish bishops, and Croke thanked him particularly. Manning confided[1] to Herbert Vaughan that he had thought his last letter would have ' vexed ' the Pope, but they had been ' on the brink of an enormous scandal,' which had been due to the efforts of only a few Ministers working with Errington, unauthorized by the Cabinet. He had been thoroughly alarmed and had spared no pains to secure Dr. Walsh's appointment; not merely in the conviction that he ought to be chosen, but because of the danger to the Holy See. ' So long as the Irish people absolutely trust the Holy See in the nomination of bishops,' he wrote in retrospect, ' the faith and fidelity of the Irish people will be immutable. The day in which they begin to believe that the influence of the Protestant and anti-Catholic Government of England is felt at the Vatican in the most vital point, they will be tempted not only to mistrust, but to all manner of spiritual evils.'

One result of his intervention was to strengthen his influence with the Irish Nationalists when Gladstone came back to power and introduced his first Home Rule Bill in 1886. Manning's approval of Home Rule was well known, and his long friendship with Gladstone made him specially useful in negotiation. He was able to press for the retention of Irish members at Westminster on the ground that they would reinforce Catholic interests in England. He informed Leo XIII, in personal letters, that Davitt had insisted ' in one of his books ' that ' the presence and vigilance of Catholic M.P.s are necessary for the defence of the Faith and of the Pontiff.' Croke also[2] had assured him, he said, that the whole Irish episcopate held the

---

[1] Leslie, p. 392.   [2] Ibid., pp. 402-3.

same view, and that they considered that any measure of self-government for Ireland must provide for continued Irish representation at Westminster. But while Manning insisted upon preserving 'the integrity of the Imperial Parliament,' he was supremely anxious to avoid any appearance of lacking sympathy for Ireland. When the general election was held in the summer of 1886, which gave Parnell the 'balance of power' between Liberals and Tories, Manning warned[1] Herbert Vaughan that it would be folly for English Catholics to urge even the Catholic education question as being more important than Ireland. 'We cannot put Education before it,' he wrote. 'The Irish vote would be lost by doing so. We should seem to oppose Ireland. We should hopelessly divide our own people. We can speak on both, but not on Education alone. . . . My words will be "The integrity of the Imperial Parliament and a legislative power in Ireland for all home matters not Imperial." Also I should desire the same for Scotland and Wales.'

Gladstone's Home Rule Bill disrupted the Liberal party, and in their old age they both felt that his political career was at an end. But Parnell's agitation kept Manning constantly anxious to preserve his own influence with the Irish bishops, while the problems of the Catholics in England, who were overwhelmingly Irish, beset him always. Another opportunity of service to his friends in Ireland came with the arrival of Mgr Persico on a mission from Rome to report on complaints that the Irish clergy were condoning agrarian crime. Archbishop Croke had identified himself widely with the land agitation, and it was expected that Persico would attempt to restrain him. Manning received candid reports expressing the fears of both Croke and Walsh, and he took an opportunity to send a vigorous letter[2] to *The Times* in their defence. 'All Ireland will thank you for it,' Walsh wrote to him in June, 1887. 'It has produced an extraordinary sensation here. Few knew how thoroughly your Eminence has been with us all through this trying time.' Manning did his utmost to impress upon Persico, and also upon the Pope, that in supporting Home Rule the Irish bishops did not contemplate separation, and that Catholic influence at Westminster would not be reduced.

---

[1] Leslie, p. 408.   [2] *Ibid.*, p. 421.

But he, too, was constantly anxious that the Nationalist movement should not take a more extreme form, and he counted chiefly upon episcopal influence to restrain it.

Persico's correspondence suggests that Manning succeeded in impressing him with his own views. Manning advised the Irish bishops to show their visitor evictions in progress, if they could, or at least to let him see the desolation which evictions had caused. Walsh went to Rome in January 1888, less apprehensive than he had been, but convinced that the Pope should be directly warned of the risks of any attempt to use political influence in Anglo-Irish affairs. He wrote[1] to Manning from Naples: ' If he is prepared, in communicating with the Ministry, to put forward as essential bases of a settlement the two unchangeable requirements of Home Rule and a thoroughly satisfactory reform of our Land System, all may be well. These points are essential. No influence in the world could move our people, either at home or abroad, to abandon either one or the other.' The Pope discussed Ireland fully for hours with Walsh and the Bishop of Cork, and Walsh reported most hopefully to Manning. But a few weeks later came the Papal decree condemning William O'Brien's ' Plan of Campaign ' and the practice of boycotting. Even Persico appears not to have expected it; and Manning could only exhort the Irish bishops to fortitude and a sympathetic understanding that Rome must always proclaim principles ' in the abstract.' ' The condition of Ireland is abnormal,' Manning wrote deliberately. ' The Decree contemplates facts which do not exist.' The Government in Ireland depended entirely upon Protestant officials, supported by armed force. ' Law, order and authority may be maintained,' he wrote, ' but at the cost of violating the moral justice by which alone nations are governed. Since this Government came in, Ireland has had a Crimes Act, but not a remedy for one of its just complaints.'

He was eighty in 1888, and feeling the weight of years; but his spirits rose when *The Times* was exposed for having published Pigott's forged letters as evidence against Parnell, and he wrote to congratulate Parnell's counsel, Sir Charles Russell, on having ' lifted the whole subject to the level of a great national and

---

[1] Leslie, p. 424.

historical cause.' Then disaster followed, at the end of
1890, when Parnell refused to resign his leadership on being
cited in the O'Shea divorce proceedings. Manning was
consulted closely, as ever, by Walsh and the Irish bishops,
and he hoped that Parnell would allow the leadership to pass
to a committee of five. He urged Gladstone to stand firm in
refusing further co-operation with Parnell as leader, but to
persevere indomitably with his plans for Home Rule. He
even sent Walsh an Address to the Irish People, but the
Archbishop wisely delayed its publication and eventually
suppressed it, informing Manning that he was already sus-
pected in Ireland of having instigated both Gladstone and the
Irish party to throw over Parnell. But Manning in England
could feel glad that the disastrous ' split ' in the nationalist
forces had re-asserted the influence of the Irish clergy. To
W. T. Stead he wrote at the end of 1890: ' For ten years
Ireland has been dragged by the politicians. It will now, I
hope, return to its old guides.'

In the previous year, 1889, he had shown what astonishing
influence even in London could be exercised by a Catholic
bishop, when he was invoked to settle the great dock strike
which had paralysed the port for months and frustrated all
attempts to end it. His intervention had succeeded, by his
personal prestige as a champion of social justice, and more
directly because of his following among the Irish Catholic
dockers. Three years before, in 1886, he had written[1] to
Archbishop Walsh:

> In the time of my predecessor there was a great breach
> between English and Irish Catholics. For twenty years I
> have laboured to heal it. It is unhappily again open. But
> the English Catholics are few. The mass of our people are
> Irish and united with Ireland. Michael Davitt first sug-
> gested to me the risk of losing forty or fifty Catholic members
> from the Imperial Parliament. It is obvious. It is a
> Catholic and a world-wide danger. I hope justice will
> reign in Ireland without that danger.

That hope was not to be fulfilled. But his achievement in
settling the London dock strike brought him an unexpected
consolation during the last few years, when he reflected upon

---

[1] Leslie, p. 415.

his life's work and set down his thoughts for the guidance of his successors.

On November 9, 1890, he wrote the last entry in his diary, after an interval of six months during which he had been steadily writing 'in another MS book,' at the request of Herbert Vaughan. 'There is one thought, I may say fact, that has come before me,' he wrote, 'and I wish to note it. I remember how often I have said that my chief sacrifice in becoming Catholic was "that I ceased to work for the people of England, and had thenceforward to work for the Irish occupation in England." Strangely all this is reversed. If I had not become Catholic I could never have worked for the people of England, as in the last year they think I have worked for them.'

IX

MANNING AND THE WORKERS

By John Fitzsimons

ONE day during the great Dock Strike of 1889 the leaders of the strike began to falter. In particular, Ben Tillett was discouraged by the fact that some of the men were drifting back to work and wanted to call a halt. He was prevailed on by Tom Mann to hold on for another day, and on this understanding went off to his lodging in a side-street in Poplar. When he arrived he was told by his landlady that there was a priest in the kitchen who had been waiting for him all afternoon. He went in and found the priest reading the latest adventure of Sherlock Holmes in the *Strand Magazine*. He looked up and Tillett saw that it was the eighty-one year old Cardinal Manning. The Cardinal had come for news of the strike, and asked how much longer the men could stay out and if they were in a ' state of grace.' Tillett said he did not know about the grace, but the men were certainly in a state of hunger. The following day the Cardinal offered his services as a mediator, and eventually was largely instrumental in getting the dockers their ' tanner.' This was the crowning act of those latter years of his life which he had devoted to working for the poor and the oppressed.

In his Anglican days he had been so involved in the theological controversies of the day that he had not been part of the growing social consciousness in the Church of England. Just as he did not consider himself part of the Oxford Movement, so he too held aloof from those Broad Churchmen, like Maurice and Kingsley, who were earning for themselves the name of ' Christian Socialists.' Nevertheless he was not insensible to the conditions under which many of his parishioners in Lavington lived, and was later to recall that ' for seventeen years I sat day by day in the homes of the labouring men of Sussex, and I knew them all and their children by name as well as I knew the scantiness of their means of subsistence.' During the hungry forties he dwelt more than once in his Charges on the rights of labour, and in one such Charge he wrote: ' It is a high sin in the sight of heaven for a man to wring his wealth out of the thews and sinews of his fellows, and to think that when he has paid them their wages he has paid them all he owes.' Nevertheless, it was not a dominant preoccupation, neither then nor for many years to come. In fact one may say that Manning did not really turn his mind to the ' social question ' until after the Vatican Council when, in his sixties, he was at the height of his powers and of his triumphs. He had never forgotten the poor of his diocese and of the country at large—he refused to do more than buy a site for a new cathedral and justified himself with the question, ' Could I leave twenty thousand children without education and drain my friends to pile up stones and bricks? '

Manning never let his other interests completely smother his solicitude for the poor, their housing conditions, their education, their temptations and their rights. Knowing the evils that drink had wrought among so many of them who found in it the only escape from the gruelling drabness of their work and the sordid overcrowded nature of their surroundings, he gave himself wholeheartedly to the temperance campaign, and was always willing to appear and speak for the League of the Cross. He himself had founded the League, after seeing for himself in the slums off Drury Lane the terrible effects of drunkenness, and it was his special interest to the end of his life. One may say that it was through the League that he first made contact with the people. The leaders of the League came every week to Archbishop's House to report their progress, and through these meetings he acquired an intimate knowledge of the life and problems of the ordinary working man in London. It brought him to the masses, too, because he spoke at many open air meetings at Hyde Park, Trafalgar Square, Tower Hill, Clerkenwell Green and London Fields. He was at his ease with such audiences and was popular because of his quiet humour. He recognized that this had made him a popular and accepted figure when he noted in 1890: ' The League has taken hold of the people, especially the working men. It was this that gave me a hold in the Strike of last year, not only of my own men but also of the Englishmen, who were as two to one.'

J

However, his first entry into the public exercise of social charity was as a member of the Committee of the Mansion House French Relief Fund during the Franco-Prussian War of 1870-1. From then on there were very few charitable works launched at Mansion House, the centre of philanthropic endeavours, which did not include the Archbishop of Westminster as a member of the committee, and as a forceful advocate of their cause. In fact anybody who had a genuine social reform to advocate or a scheme for helping the needy and downtrodden was always sure of a welcome at Archbishop's House—all that is except the supporters of equal rights for women whom he consistently refused to receive. He showed great sympathy and understanding with the first efforts of the Salvation Army.

> The Salvation Army [he wrote] could never have existed but for the spiritual desolation of England . . . it would surely be within the truth to say that half the population of London are practically without God in the world. If this be so, then at once we can see how and why the Salvation Army exists. Throughout the provinces of England, there are millions living without faith and in sin. To such a people a voice crying aloud in God's name is as a warning in the night. . . . A watchman's rattle is good at night. . . . Our heart's desire and prayer is that they who labour so fervently with the truths they know may be led into the fulness of faith.

His position was confirmed when he was appointed a member of the Royal Commission on the Housing of the Working Classes in March 1884. The Secretary of the Commission was moved to say that ' if there had been half a dozen Mannings England would have run some risk of being converted to Christianity.' Once the Commission had reported and legislation passed he was impatient that changes did not come more quickly.

> We are baffled [he said at a Mansion House conference on the housing of the poor, in June 1885] by the interests of those who own the houses, and baffled by the inertness of those who ought to put the Statutes into force. . . . If only those in London who have heads and hearts to care for the condition of the poor, and who have been aroused within

the last six months to the consciousness of an intolerable evil, would continue and maintain this movement by their self-denying efforts, I believe there would be found the dynamic force that would put the law into operation; and then gradually and with patience, with these kindly and generous modes of treatment with which alone human affairs can be governed, we shall find a full and complete remedy for these sufferings of the population.

His approach to the social problem was one of intellectual conviction, and although he was not without human feelings (even sharing the family heritage of ' Berserker ' rages) he never allowed his emotions to take command. Herein lay his great strength as a social reformer. The emotional man who lets his heart run away with his head may become a successful demagogue, but he can never command the respect and the assent of thinking men. In the Gorham case Manning had relentlessly used the tests of law and logic to see whether ' the Church of England be a divine or human society.' It was said of him, in this instance, that he applied canon law ' like arguments from pure mathematics.' So too, when he repeated the words of his Master, ' *Misereor super turbam*,' he did not let his pity degenerate into sentiment or mere philanthropy—on the contrary he looked for lasting and structural changes in society. He denounced three plagues which were destroying the people:

(1) The Land Laws since the Reformation.

(2) The Relations of Capital and Labour during the last hundred years of selfish Political Economy.

(3) The Drink Trade, which had been fostered by capitalists and favoured by the Government for the sake of revenue.

He said, ' Keep inviolate the commonwealth of England, but destroy these three gangrenes which are inevitably destroying its life—that is, the human and domestic life of the people—for the enrichment of a handful of capitalists and landowners.'

Both as a citizen and as a churchman he welcomed the changes that he foresaw:

Politicians and political economists of the modern school have had their day. The twentieth century will be the day of the people. . . . The coming age will belong neither to the capitalists nor to the commercial classes, but to the

People. . . . If we can gain their confidence we can counsel them; if we show them a blind opposition they will have power to destroy all that is good. . . . But I hope much from the action of the Church. . . . her true home is with the People.

Once he was convinced that the Trade Unions were a necessary instrument for the workers he gave them his full support. As early as 1874, when the semi-skilled and unskilled workers were as yet unorganized and the Unions had not received their legal charter, he said:

It would seem to me that the protection of labour and of industry has at all times been a recognized right of those who possess the same craft; that they have united together; that those unions have been recognized by the legislature; that whether they be employers or employed . . . all have the same rights. And I do not see, I confess, why all men should not organize themselves together, so long as they are truly and honestly submissive to one higher and chief, who is superior over us all—the supreme reign of law which has governed, at all times, the people of England.

This statement came at the end of a brief survey of the history of trade associations, guilds and unions where, characteristically, he had confessed that a certain book, Brentano on Guilds, ' took out of my mind entirely the erroneous conception which in some degree I had formed, that such associations have anything about them which is not perfectly innocuous if they are rightly conducted.'

Although he was in constant touch with the men who were fighting to establish the new unions, there were three occasions when he entered the lists publicly on their behalf. The first time was to help Joseph Arch in his struggle to found the National Agricultural Labourers' Union, and to demand the vote for them. He spoke at a public meeting at the Exeter Hall in 1872, and again in 1874, where other speakers were Sir Charles Dilke and Sir Charles Trevelyan. He had been invited to chair the meeting but declined because he thought it might be detrimental to the interests of the Union to have a Catholic Archbishop presiding. But he did move the first Resolution, and claimed some right to speak because of his seventeen years at Lavington. He went on to call for ' the amendment of the land laws in England and the reconstitution of the domestic life of the labouring poor.' When later criticized he defended himself and Joseph Arch.

> To couple my name with that of Mr. Arch gives me no displeasure. I believe him to be an honest and good man. I believe, too, that the cause he has in hand is well founded; and I confide in his using no means to promote it but such as are sanctioned by the law of God and the law of the land.

Arch, in his turn, left it on record that Manning 'spoke up nobly for us. The testimony at such a time and in such a place of a man so respected was of the greatest value to the Union.'

Manning followed up his attendance at the meeting by writing to Gladstone:

> Why cannot you do these things for the labourer? Prohibit the labour of children under a certain age. Compel payment of wages in money. Regulate the number of dwellings according to the population of parishes. Establish tribunals of arbitration in counties for questions between labour and land.

And, not forgetting the conditions of the farm workers in Kent and Sussex, he showed his practical support for the Union by contributing to its funds, in 1878 and 1879. He had always felt too that the land question was at the heart of the Irish Question and in his letter to Earl Grey in 1868 (to which he referred frequently in after years) he had suggested reforms in the land laws which would mitigate hardships and remove the injustices which left the Irish peasant a prey to extremists.

> The Land Question [he wrote] means hunger, thirst, nakedness, notice to quit, labour spent in vain, the toil of years seized upon, the breaking up of homes, the miseries, the sickness, deaths of parents, children, wives; the despair and wildness which spring up in the hearts of the poor when legal force, like a sharp harrow, goes over the most sensitive and vital right of mankind. All this is contained in the land question.

The next connection that Manning had with the Trade Union movement was much more important and had worldwide repercussions. In 1870 a workers' organization called the Knights of Labour had been founded in the U.S.A. and by the middle of the eighties, due to the generalship of T. V. Powderley, counted many thousands of members in all the industrial areas in the eastern and mid-western states. It had spread to Canada and was there condemned as a secret society in 1886 by the Archbishop of Quebec, Cardinal Taschereau, who excommunicated its members for their revolutionary programme which contained, among other points, a demand for the nationalization of the mines and railways. A general condemnation was being prepared in Rome, at the instance of Cardinal Taschereau, and Cardinal Gibbons was despatched post haste as the spokesman of the American bishops to prevent its promulgation. In the compelling case that he put forward for the Knights of Labour he was supported by Cardinal Manning, whom he had consulted, along with President Cleveland, as soon as he got wind of the proposed action of the Holy Office. Manning wrote:

Up to the present the world has been governed by dynasties: henceforward the Holy See must treat with the people, and with bishops who are in close daily and personal relations with the people. The more this is clearly and fully acknowledged, the more firmly will the exercise of spiritual authority be established. Never in past times was the Hierarchy so free of hindrance from civil power, so mutually responsible, so united with the Holy See as at present. To recognize this evident fact and turn it to account means power; to neglect it, or not to perceive it, would lead to endless confusion. This is the opportunity of the present. The Church is the Mother, Friend, and Protectress of the People. As our Divine Saviour lived among persons of the people, so lives His Church. On this point the Cardinal's argument is irresistible. I trust that before leaving Rome he may clearly discover to all this New World, the World of the Future.

It is clear that Cardinal Gibbons followed out Manning's wishes, for in the statement which he presented to the Congregation of Propaganda on February 20, 1887, he wrote:

And since it is acknowledged by all that the great questions of the future are not those of war, of commerce or finance, but the social questions, the questions which concern the

improvement of the condition of the great masses of the
people, and especially of the working people, it is evidently
of supreme importance that the Church should always be
found on the side of humanity, of justice toward the
multitudes who compose the body of the human family.
As the same Cardinal Manning [he had previously quoted
him] very wisely wrote, ' We must admit and accept calmly
and with good will that industries and profits must be
considered in second place; the moral state and domestic
condition of the whole working population must be considered first. I will not venture to formulate the acts of
parliament, but here is precisely their fundamental principle
for the future. The conditions of the lower classes as are
found at present among our people, can not and must not
continue. On such a basis no social edifice can stand.'

The result was that the condemnation was scrapped, Cardinal
Taschereau was instructed to withdraw the excommunication,
and Manning's position as the friend and the protector of
the workingman was enhanced both in England and in the
United States and Canada.

But his greatest act was still to come: the part he played
in the settlement of the London Dock Strike of 1889, when
he was in his eighty-second year. For some time before this
Manning had been in contact with the leaders of the New
Unionism, and in particular with Ben Tillett, who bore witness
that in Manning's constant encouragement he found the
strength to persevere in organizing the Gas-workers' Union.
Early in August 1889 this Union felt strong enough to demand
an eight-hour day. After a delay, but without a struggle,
this was granted. This success determined Tillett to try and
do something for the casual dock workers of the Port of London.
An insignificant dispute provided the occasion, and within
three days ten thousand dockers, led by Tillett, Tom Mann
and John Burns, had left the precarious, dangerous and ill-
paid work for which, morning after morning, they had fought
at the dock gates. They demanded an extra penny an hour
(making it up to sixpence, the ' tanner '), the abolition of sub-
contract and piece-work, extra pay for overtime, and a minimum engagement of four hours. The Dock Directors refused
to discuss the matter and, because their attempts to import
' blackleg ' labour had been frustrated by public opinion, for

four weeks the Port of London lay idle. So long as the Directors remained unmoved, the deadlock could not be broken. Despite generous public subscriptions for the dockers and their families, to which contributions came from as far away as Australia, it was clear that soon starvation would stalk through the tenement homes of the East End. Moreover, although the strikers had behaved in an orderly fashion, there was the ever-present danger of disorder and riot which could do incalculable harm to property (Manning thought particularly of the ravages of fire in the warehouse areas) and might mean the loss of many lives.

Manning's way was clear. Writing later, in a commentary on *Rerum Novarum*, he showed the considerations that moved him to intervene. ' If Parliament is not assembled and danger is urgent, it is the right and duty of every loyal man, who loves his country and his people, at any cost or danger to himself, to come between the parties in conflict, and to bring them, if he can, to peace.' Feeling it to be no less than his duty, he went to see the Directors but made little headway with what he subsequently called an ' impenitent congregation.'

A committee of reconciliation was then formed which included the Lord Mayor, the Bishop of London and the Cardinal. One of the committee, Mr. Sydney (afterwards Lord) Buxton, the Member of Parliament for Poplar, speaking of the part played by the Cardinal noted how ' day after day from ten in the morning till seven or eight at night he spent interviewing, discussing, negotiating. . . . He was always confident that with time, tact and patience, peace would speedily prevail.' Tillett appreciated how he ' chided the pomp of the Lord Mayor, the harshness of Temple (Bishop of London), the pushfulness of Burns.' Eventually the ' tanner ' was agreed to, and all that remained was to discuss the date when it would come into operation and for the men to agree to return to work immediately. At this point the men repudiated their negotiators, and the committee of reconciliation withdrew in disgust. The Cardinal alone remained and went down to Poplar to meet the strikers' committee. For two hours, in Wade Street School, the discussion went on without any sign of the men agreeing to compromise. Then the Cardinal played his trump. He threatened to address the strikers himself and to call on the Catholics, a very large proportion, to follow his advice. He had won—forty-two out of the forty-five present voted to empower Manning to inform the Directors that they were willing to compromise on the date. Two days later an agreement was signed and the dockers returned to work. To commemorate the event the men collected £160 which they presented to Manning; with it Manning endowed a bed in the London Hospital. The settlement of the Dock Strike was the crowning act of his long and varied career, and the Press commented that he had gained the Primacy of England not, one is tempted to add, from the hands of Gladstone but from the workers of the East End. The following year, when the first May Day processions were held in London, several banners bore portraits of Marx and Manning, side by side!

In the last twenty years of his life Manning expressed his social philosophy in lectures given in Mechanics' Institutes in various industrial cities, in articles published in English and American reviews, and in vigorous letters to correspondents in England, Europe and America. *The Times* occasionally carried a column-long letter from his pen, and indeed he once wrote a letter that was so long that it was published in two parts on two consecutive days. His fundamental proposition was that work was a human thing, and that people were more important than production. He expressed this most eloquently in his speech on 'The Dignity and Rights of Labour,' at Leeds in 1874.

If the great end of life were to multiply yards of cloth and cotton twist, and if the glory of England consists or consisted in multiplying, without stint or limit, these articles and the like at the lowest possible price, so as to undersell all the nations of the world, well, then, let us go on. But if the domestic life of the people be vital above all; if the peace, the purity of homes, the education of children, the duties of wives and mothers, the duties of husbands and fathers, be written in the natural law of mankind, and if these things are sacred, far beyond anything that can be sold in the market— then I say, if the hours of labour resulting from the un- regulated sale of a man's strength and skill shall lead to the destruction of domestic life, to the neglect of children, to turning wives and mothers into living machines, and of

K

fathers and husbands into—what shall I say—creatures of burden—I will not use any other word—who rise up before the sun, and come back when it is set, wearied and able only to take food and to lie down to rest—the domestic life of men exists no longer, and we dare not go on in this path.

From this central idea of the value of the human person developed a further idea which Manning repeated again and again, that the labour, strength and skill of the worker is capital, 'live capital.' He contrasted this with the other factors of production and called them ' dead capital,' for they only receive their life from the living power and skill of the worker.

Labour and skill are Capital as much as gold and silver. Labour and skill can produce without gold and silver. Gold and silver are dependent on Labour and skill, but Labour and skill are independent *in limine*. The union of the two Capitals demands participation in the product. Wages are a minimized money representation of shares in the product—that is, in profits. . . .   Individualism, selfishness, freedom of contract, and competition, have obliterated the first principles of the Metayer System.

As for the dignity of labour:

It is the law of our state, the law of our development and perfection, the source of invention, the power of creation, and the cause of manifold capital in money and in skill. And as to its rights . . . it is true property, true capital . . . it has a primary right of freedom, a right to protect itself, and a claim upon the law of the land to protect it.

But Labour, he said, was being robbed of its rights. The whole capitalist system was organized in such an uncontrolled way that justice was flouted. ' There is no justice, mercy or compassion in the Plutocracy. There is my creed.'

It is not surprising that after making statements like that he was accused of being a Socialist. He knew this, but did not modify his opinions.

We have been, up to now, hampered by an excessive individualism [he wrote to the Editor of the *XXième Siècle*] and the next century will show that mankind is greater and more noble than any individual thing. This doctrine, which has its foundation upon Nature's law and Christianity, is taxed with being Socialistic by thoughtless and rash people, as well as by capitalists and the wealthy. But the future will see the light of reason shed upon the social state of the labouring world.

He insisted that the worker had, in justice, a claim to a share of the end-product of the industrial process, a share which he takes in the form of wages. His point was that since the coming of Industrialism the worker had rarely, if ever, been given his just share.

> During a hundred years the capitalist has wilfully concealed the enormous amount of his profits, and has meanwhile been buying labour at the lowest rate possible. . . . The absolute obstacle at the present moment is the refusal of capitalists to reveal their profits.

At a time when the *laisser-faire* tradition still dominated the thinking of economists and politicians alike, he boldly demanded Government intervention for the regulation of hours and the establishment of a fixed minimum wage. If possible, he wanted these matters arranged by discussion between organized workers and organized employers.

> They ought freely to confer, face to face, in any contention arising between them; and, failing to agree, they ought to refer their contention to councils of conciliation freely chosen by each side. If these should finally fail to bring peace, society at large may protect itself by spontaneous intervention, or, last of all, by the authority of legislation.

He was a member of the Committee that brought into being the London Conciliation Board, and was on friendly terms with its first chairman, and through him followed the actions of the Board with sympathetic interest.

Today this suggestion, and others that he made, are the common currency of industrial relations, and it is difficult to understand how severely and bitterly Manning was criticized. There were even some, highly-placed churchmen among them, who excused his views on the grounds of senility. But then the same was said of Pope Leo XIII when he issued the encyclical *Rerum Novarum*. With the publication of this encyclical in May 1891, Manning felt he could sing his *Nunc Dimittis*, and in fact he died seven months later. It justified the stand that he had taken, and indeed whole phrases seemed to echo his own writings and pronouncements. He wrote, in the *Dublin Review*, a commentary on it which he regarded as his 'last social testament.' The article shows that, though he was now in his eighty-fourth year, he still preserved his incisive clarity of thought and vigour of expression.

> If any man would protect the world of labour from the oppression of 'free contracts' or 'starvation wages,' he is a Socialist. So obscure from want of thought, or so warped by interest, or so prejudiced by class feeling are the minds of men.

One cannot help feeling that this shaft was aimed at, among others, *The Times*. Against this newspaper he waged constant wa¬, partly because of its anti-papal policy and partly because it was so antipathetic to his economic and social convictions. Once when it attacked him for denying the validity of the *laisser-faire* economists' solution to unemployment, he ended his reply with the waspish sentence: ' It may be needless to waste time upon me; but your time would not be wasted in finding a prompt and adequate relief for the present and urgent distress of thousands of our best and worthiest working men, with their wives and children. Hitherto this has not been done by *The Times*.'

His death was mourned by all the working people of London. In an address presented to him after the Dock Strike they had spoken of him as ' a father in the midst of a loving and well-loved family.' It was as such that they felt their loss. They had known his charity, which some had criticized for being indiscriminate. But he had said, ' I am content that many unworthy should share rather than one worthy case be without help.' Above all they had known him as the champion of their rights, and had been heartened by his inflexible desire for justice. The charity of Christ was his, giving him compassion on the multitude, impelling him to go about doing good, earning for him from friend and foe alike the honourable title of ' Friend of the People.'

X

MANNING THE SPIRITUAL WRITER

By H. Francis Davis

WE have at Oscott College a painting of the First Provincial Synod of the restored Hierarchy, held in our chapel in 1852, on which Newman and Manning can be seen seated side by side. I have never heard any visitor express surprise at this. We do tend rather to couple their names together. Unfortunately, more often than not, we couple them in order to contrast them. When writing or speaking of one, we feel that some explanation is required of their failure to understand each other, and of their difference of character and vocation. Though no one doubts that Newman's was the greater genius, Manning is recognized to have possessed qualities which enabled him to succeed where Newman would have failed. Manning's qualities were most strikingly in the practical and administrative order, and future generations forget gifts which so little concern them. Apart from personal sanctity, which, when it is known and outstanding, continues to impress posterity, future generations judge a man's greatness chiefly by the works of literature or art or by any other monument he leaves to the world.

As a writer and thinker Newman stands alone, and he was at no time more widely or deeply appreciated than he is today. Manning clearly could never hope to have the same following. But he has a following; and many of his writings, especially those which might be classed as 'spiritual reading,' are still read and valued. True, they do not provoke intense critical study, they are not notable for their originality, they are rarely quoted in the schools, and little known among non-Catholics. We must not conclude that we owe little or nothing to these works. I hope to show that Manning's spiritual writing may have been as important as, say, his social work, or any other of his achievements.

Newman and Manning were both prophets to their age. They witnessed to truths little known or appreciated in their time, and yet highly valued and widely recognized today. Newman was the more creative. His work was a new beginning, in the sense that our recognition of the truths he stood for is almost exclusively due to him, and without him we might still be ignorant. Manning discerned the coming reaction against naturalistic tendencies within the Church, and preached grace and the supernatural to Catholics who had been so much affected by their century that they did not realize that grace and the supernatural were fast losing their true Catholic meaning. This reaction against nineteenth-century naturalism would undoubtedly have come whether or not Manning had spoken and written, but he was destined to play a vital part in preparing English-speaking Catholics for a newer and more Catholic emphasis.

Each had a prophetic intuition of some of the grave problems of his time, and each as an apostle of truth offered his solution. The problems they dealt with and therefore the solutions they offered were in different spheres. There were more ways than one in which Victorians were drifting from the truth. Newman thought that the challenge of rationalism, atheism and indifferentism was the most dangerous. Manning was more anxious about the Catholics who were not Catholics; Catholics who no longer knew the Spirit and His work within them, or had forgotten that the Church is God dwelling among men; Catholics who were so ready to appear friendly to their fellow-countrymen that they were in danger of compromising the divine truths of the faith. Newman wrote of truth to people who no longer sought it. Manning wrote of the doctrines of our faith to people who accepted them without hesitation, but did not realize they had to live by them. Newman appealed to the whole man, intellect, heart and imagination; and devoted all his powers to win wholehearted conviction. Manning in his spiritual writings is less interested in proving, and he rarely considers the objections of rationalists or other non-Catholics. He is satisfied to use every device to bring home to his listeners what they can find proved elsewhere, if they wish, though in any case they probably will not wish. Manning has occasionally been adversely criticized for this ' dogmatic ' or ' unscientific ' approach, but unfairly; since a man must be judged by the object he sets himself, and in these writings theology or apologetics fall outside his end.

It was inevitable that in preparing this essay I should look for some principle of unity. Sometimes it is hard to discover any unity in a man's writings on any subject. The layman is inclined to think that a man's writings arise out of special occasions, and for this reason he is suspicious that the unity that is later ' found ' in them has been rather imposed by its discoverer. In actual fact it is probable that all writers unconsciously tend to continue along certain lines of thought, and the more influential the writer the more noticeable this is. In the case of Manning fortunately all his spiritual writing is fired by one inspiration, to bring home to clergy and laity a vivid sense of the supernatural reality of the Church and what this involves in her individual members. Failure to realize God's presence in the Church, sacraments and inner spiritual life of the Christian was seen by Manning to be the dominant fault of non-Catholics of his century. Catholics themselves had been only too often affected by this naturalistic outlook of the world around them. At a memorable conference given before the Annual Meeting of the Newman Association in Birmingham, 1950, Father M. C. D'Arcy, S.J., thrilled his audience with his account of the momentous growth of knowledge and appreciation of our supernatural life and of our membership of the Mystical Body, among Catholics of our own generation. He showed how lacking people had been in their understanding of these Christian truths as little time back as the first decades of this century. And yet Cardinal Manning, a generation or two still earlier, wrote almost exclusively on these subjects that today mean so much. The basic thesis of his purely spiritual writings is given in the work *The Temporal Mission of the Holy Ghost*. Here he deals with the Holy Ghost dwelling in Christ and after Christ in Christ's Body, the Church. The internal hallowing presence of the Spirit changing what is natural into a vessel of the supernatural is shown in its meaning for the individual soul in the work *The Internal Mission of the Holy Ghost*.

If there be one thing that is to our shame, one thing which ought to cast us down with our faces in the dust, it is this:

that we live all the day long as if there were no Holy Ghost, as if we were like the Ephesians who, when the Apostle asked them if they had received the Holy Ghost since they believed, said: ' We have not so much as heard whether there be a Holy Ghost.' We live in the world and are worldly; we live on the earth and of the earth are earthy; we live for pleasure, we live for trade, for money, for levities, for frivolities, for the indulgence of our own will.

God is the life of the soul, and people forget both God and soul and live for the body. That is the modern tragedy. Is there any life for the soul apart from God? It was normal not long ago for theologians to think that there could have been a life of the soul without the supernatural, if God had chosen to leave us without His grace. Recently the well-known French Jesuit, Father de Lubac, has been defending the view that not only is the supernatural the only actual end for which God made us, but that further our nature is such that it never could find happiness in a purely natural end. Father de Lubac claims that this was the normal view until the close of the thirteenth century. Manning knew nothing of this modern controversy, but he always seems to suppose the position defended by Father de Lubac as normal. ' The body hungers and thirsts for its natural food; the soul after God, Who is the breath of its life, its sole and only sustenance. Its desire becomes more and more intense as God is more and more known and appreciated.'

For Manning, then, to be uninterested in grace and the Holy Spirit is to live for the body. ' The greater part of men live as if they had no souls.' Faith, Hope, Charity and the Gifts are necessary for the perfect life of the soul, which consists in knowing the truth about God and itself on the only authority who can be trusted in such matters, that of God; also in realizing that God is our end and seeking Him; and lastly in living in perfect friendship with Him. This supernatural life demands the Gifts of the Holy Ghost, those special enlightenments given by the Spirit enabling us to understand the things of God, see them as God sees them, act divinely in difficult circumstances, in the way that God would like us to act; and to do all this with proper filial fear, the devotion of children to their Father, and complete fearlessness. Manning summarizes the place of these Gifts completing and perfecting the virtues in the following words:

> The gift of holy fear is the gift of the children of God, and the gift of piety is the gift of the sons of God, and the gift of fortitude is the gift of the soldiers of Jesus Christ, and the gift of science is the gift of the disciples of the Holy Ghost, and the gift of counsel is the gift of the pastors of the flock, and the gift of intellect is the gift of the Doctors of the Church, and the gift of wisdom is the gift of the saints, among whom are numbered little children, and all who are faithful to the Spirit of God.

In preparing this volume Manning studied the work of Denis the Carthusian. He does not seem to have been aware of the analysis of the gifts made by St Thomas and developed in the Thomist school. This is unfortunate from the point of view of the Church-student today studying the Gifts in his theology course. He inevitably turns to Manning as being an English classic on his subject. Manning's position in this is similar to that, rejected by St Thomas, of those who ' said that the gifts must be distinguished from the virtues, but did not assign any sufficient grounds of distinction, i.e., something common to the virtues not belonging to the gifts or vice versa.' St Thomas mentions several varieties of such inadequately based distinctions. Perhaps none of them quite corresponds to Manning's. Some, according to St Thomas, said that the gifts perfected the freedom as a faculty of reason, whereas the virtues perfected it as a faculty of the will. Others said that virtues were for good action, gifts for resisting temptations. Others again said that the virtues were simply for good action, while the gifts were to make us like Christ. Manning appears to regard the virtues as powers of knowing, hoping and loving; and the gifts as springs of action which elicit the operations of the virtues. He compares them to the striking of the flint which elicits fire from the flint. This description of Manning's could no doubt without much difficulty be adapted to St Thomas's distinction, i.e., that the virtues are internal supernatural powers of operation, and the gifts powers enabling the Holy Ghost to teach and inspire us from without as to when and how we should use our virtues. Manning's whole analysis would have been greatly clarified and deepened if he had been conscious, and made his readers conscious, that they are not just superior heroic virtues, but rather a type of super-natural docility or wakefulness to the voice and inspiration of the Holy Spirit. Apart from this, there is something of permanent value in Manning's own account of what each gift contributes to our spiritual life, and immense profit can still be gained from its careful reading.

Another aspect of the divine Church, flowing from Christ and never separated from Christ, was the Incarnation itself. So it entered into Manning's scheme to write on that. This was the more especially so as he felt that even among Catholics the central doctrine of our Faith was neglected. Priests preached ethical or sentimental sermons too often, instead of preaching the Truth itself. Dogma is the Truth, the only true source of devotion. ' Without knowledge there can be no adoration " in spirit and in truth"; and just in the measure of our knowledge will our adoration be more or less perfect, that is, intelligent and spiritual. If our knowledge be full and perfect, so will our adoration be.' In case I gave the impression at the beginning of this account that Newman and Manning had little in common, let me hasten to correct this and to assert vigorously that their attitude to all these central questions is one of complete harmony. Newman was always insisting that there could be no religion without Dogma, and he was always reminding us that knowledge must precede heart and feelings, and in fact all forms of devotion.

Manning's choice of title, *The Glories of the Sacred Heart*, came from the popularity of that devotion in his time, as well as from a genuine conviction that no other devotion would do more to foster true ideas of God, Christ and religion. He claimed that ' the knowledge of the Sacred Heart is the most perfect of dogmas: that it contains in itself the knowledge of God, the knowledge of man, the knowledge of the sanctifica-tion of our humanity in Jesus Christ, and therefore of our own sanctification. It sets before us an example of all perfection, and of our relations to God and to one another.' The applica-tion of the Incarnation to our souls through the Eucharist forms a great part of his volume. There are two ways to learn wisdom from Christ's Sacred Heart, from the living voice of the Church and from Christ directly in the Blessed Sacrament.

There is perhaps no better token of Manning's ability to feel himself into the popular doctrines of a future generation, and realize before the mass of Christians the meaning of the hidden depths of our Faith than his anticipation by some forty or fifty years of the devotion to Christ the King. This is in his chapter on the *Temporal Glory of the Sacred Heart.*

> The outward life and the inward Heart of our Divine Redeemer have become the pattern and law to men. And as the world was changed in individuals, households, and kingdoms, the Church of God became the mother and queen of the nations. . . . But Jesus not only reigns personally among men, by an outward sovereignty; He reigns also by an inward sovereignty, by the inflexibility of justice over the will, and by the infallibility of truth over the intellect and the conscience of men—over those that believe, for their joy and their salvation; over those that will not believe, for their peril and for their sentence hereafter. . . . The Incarnate Word dethroned the world. Its atheism, its idolatries, its cruelties, its immoralities, its philosophies, its superstitions, were all swept away in the light of the Incarnation; but ever since its downfall the world has been striving to dethrone the Incarnate Word.

The practical application of this compendium of Incarnation, Eucharist and Headship of Christ is that we should regard our process of sanctification as a modelling of ourselves according to the pattern of Christ, under the symbol of His Sacred Heart. Making our hearts conform to the Sacred Heart is the only way of holiness for all.

Manning's little book of Lenten sermons on *Sin and its Consequences* underlines all he says elsewhere about the supreme importance of keeping our hearts at all times open to the work of the Holy Ghost. A great part of the books we have just been considering concerns the freedom of man and the capacity man possesses for ruining God's work in the soul by sin or failure to co-operate. In this Lenten book, he is able to make this the main burden of his argument. In connection with this, we find another connecting link with Newman in his vivid realization of the possibility of secret sins, which ruin us, and yet we do nothing about them, since we are not aware of them.

> Every day of your life pray God to give you light to see yourselves just as He sees you now: to show you what sin is in all its hideousness, in all its subtilty, and to show you those secret sins which you do not see yourselves. Every day of your life ask this of God.

I suppose the most popular of all Manning's spiritual works is his *Eternal Priesthood*. This work caught the imagination of the Catholic world and was translated into many European languages. Manning himself was always very diffident—unjustly so, most people think—about his powers as a writer, and he did not think his works would long survive his death. But he derived consolation from the widespread and continuing success of this work, which was obviously nearest to his heart. Few Church students since Manning's time have failed to be inspired by it. It would be hard to find another work on the priesthood regarded with equal reverence, unless it be one of the classics of antiquity. Everything in it was written to impress indelibly upon his reader that, in this divine institution on earth, the Church of Christ, hallowed and guided by the Holy Spirit, ' there can be conceived no office higher, and no power greater, than the office and power of the priest.' If only the student could become firmly and finally convinced of this, there would be little need for other rules of conduct. It is rather like the saying of St Augustine: ' Love God, and do what you like.' Manning might almost have said: ' Know what it is to be a priest and follow your inclinations.' He did not say that, nor would he have done, because he did not trust the capacity of the ordained priest never to forget what he is.

> In the order of divine actions it places the priest, in respect to the power of consecration, next to the Blessed Virgin, the living tabernacle of the Incarnate Word; and, in respect to the guardianship of the Blessed Sacrament, next to St Joseph, the foster-father and guardian of the Son of God.

He supports his position with frequent references to the great patristic and later treatises on this subject, notably to

St John Chrysostom, St Basil, St Gregory, St Augustine, St Thomas and St Charles.

He draws one paramount—though somewhat controversial—conclusion from this. A priest—like a bishop—is in a state of pefection. He complained that this claim was made by Religious, whether priests or laymen, but was too often surrendered by the secular clergy. This led to a view the contrary of the truth. The secular priest is actually more bound to perfection than the unordained religious. Manning's position has been defended eloquently in recent times by Canon E. J. Mahoney, in his masterly work on *The Secular Priesthood*. An ascetical and educational consequence of such a view would be that students to the secular priesthood must be made to realize their positive duty of attaining perfection before being ordained. This perfection does not mean that they must be perfect in the full sense of the term, but that they must be ready to die rather than commit a grave sin, and that they must dedicate themselves completely to their priestly work and their personal growth in holiness. This gives us the second consequence. A priest is obliged to persevere after his ordination in the state of perfection.

The success of the book—as of most of Manning's books—lies in the fact that he never stops short at stating his thesis speculatively, hoping that the glory of the doctrine and the grace of God will do the rest. Like all great preachers, he is anxious to translate his principles into everyday life. He is like Newman here in the task he sets before him, but unlike him in its method of accomplishment. Both are practical, but in different ways. Both wish to translate abstract truths into concrete life. Newman does so by revealing to his listeners what is going on in their souls, and bringing them to see the only logical remedy. Manning has not such a gift of reading men's souls. But he knows the main psychological truths of mankind as a whole, and on these lines it is easy for him to show the young priest how he can set about 'living' his priesthood.

There are of course means of perfection inherent in the priestly state and pastoral life. He is directly united to the Great High Priest, the origin of all our holiness. He is the custodian of the Blessed Sacrament, the principal instrument

of holiness and communion with God. He is the vocational
pastor of his flock, bound by his calling to be always striving
after the sanctity of others.   How can all this fail to have a deep
and sincere influence upon his own holiness, his own response
to grace ?   Going more into details, Manning reminds the
priest what he can gain from the daily recital of his Divine
Office.   More important than this is his daily offering of the
Sacred Victim at Mass. ' He is our food, our shelter, our
refreshment, our delight, and our evergrowing strength.'
' The whole Church is the sanctuary, and the Divine Office
is the ritual of the choir on earth uniting with the praises,
thanksgivings, and doxologies which are the ritual of the choir
in heaven.   Every priest has his place in this choir, and he
makes seven visits to the heavenly court day by day.'   With
his Mass and Office he has the daily mental prayer, to which he
is bound. ' This enables him to realize the objects of faith,
of the world unseen as if it were visible, and of the future as
if it were present.'   Newman lovers will recognize in this
last sentence an echo of one of the most inspiring of the parochial sermons.

   But there are many and serious dangers for a man leading so
supernatural a life in a world that has forgotten the meaning
and existence of the divine order.   He must beware of worldly
consolations, especially when the freshness is beginning to wear
off.   He must beware of routine and professionalism.   He
must even beware of having his spiritual and intellectual life destroyed by excess of activity.   Manning in this is touching upon
a commonplace of all spiritual writing since the beginning,
the seemingly unanswerable problem of how to do the overwhelming mass of work which is thrust on one, and yet preserve
enough leisure and calmness of mind to give oneself regularly
in silent union of prayer with God.   A difficulty felt keenly
by Manning was the danger of preaching ostentatiously,
merely for vanity or to give pleasure.   He would have all
preaching of a style such as he sought himself in all his Catholic
works, humble and sincere, simple and straightforward.
' The preaching of the Apostles was the voice of their Divine
Master prolonged in all its majestic simplicity.'   We shall be
able to continue this if we live our sermons and preach our
lives.

It is easy to see in all this the same Cardinal Manning who had such deep and real love for the poor, who never closed his door to anyone in difficulty or want, who regarded social work done to relieve poverty as part of the duty of Christians, as part of the supernatural duty of those called to love their neighbour as Christ for Christ's sake. For this reason he was always impatient with Catholics who perhaps prided themselves on their Catholicism and yet objected to him taking part in Temperance meetings and every manner of Social Work. In this he never wavered. He knew that his duty as a Christian lay in taking practical interest, not in the rich and influential, but in those very publicans and sinners who—to the annoyance of the Pharisees—were the friends of Jesus.

He also felt strongly that, though he yielded to none in his defence of the Church as the one home of salvation, yet it is grossly wrong and most uncharitable to assert that Protestants are normally without grace and the Holy Spirit, and that they have no understanding of spiritual things. He never wavered in his conviction that untold numbers of non-Catholics retained their baptismal grace; and to this he attributed the eminent reasonableness of English public opinion in the face of the astounding and to them somewhat provoking advances of Catholics during the nineteenth century.

It was not downright atheism, he thought, or scandalous living which characterized our fellow countrymen, but rather religious confusion and a loss of a clear understanding of the Church of Christ. They must learn again to recognize ' the true and divine character of the mystical body as a creation of God, distinct from all individuals, and superior to them all: not on probation, because not dependent on any human will, but on the Divine will alone; and, therefore, not subject to human infirmity, but impeccable, and the instrument of probation to the world.' These words from his *Temporal Mission of the Holy Ghost* show why it is that the divinely ordained means of grace is found in the Church, and why priests have been given such superhuman powers to convey it from Christ the Head in the power of the Spirit to our individual souls. This is the message of Manning, a distinctive message in the time that he lived, though a common message delivered to us by all the great spiritual writers of our own generation.

Manning did his work so well that he gives us a desire to study these supernatural doctrines more deeply than in his own works. He turns us to the more developed works on the Church, the Mass, the Eucharist, Grace, the Virtues and Gifts, which are continually appearing in our Catholic world today. But nowhere do we find the simple truth of the Divine Church and its treasures of grace better introduced to us for the nourishing of our spiritual life than in the works of Manning we have been considering. Finally, whatever may be the fate of his other works, one at least, his *Eternal Priesthood*, will continue to inspire many generations of future priests. Perhaps it will remain, as those of St John Chrysostom and St Gregory, a lasting part of our Catholic heritage.